Richard Duncan Radcliffe

Schedule of Deeds and Documents

The Property of Colonel Thomas Richard Crosse Preserved in the

Muniments Room at Shaw Hill, Chorley, in the County of Lancaster

Richard Duncan Radcliffe

Schedule of Deeds and Documents
The Property of Colonel Thomas Richard Crosse Preserved in the Muniments Room at Shaw Hill, Chorley, in the County of Lancaster

ISBN/EAN: 9783337254889

Printed in Europe, USA, Canada, Australia, Japan

Cover: Foto ©Andreas Hilbeck / pixelio.de

More available books at **www.hansebooks.com**

CROSSE

DEEDS AND DOCUMENTS.

CHEDULE OF DEEDS AND DOCUMENTS, THE PROPERTY OF COLONEL THOMAS RICHARD CROSSE, PRESERVED IN THE MUNIMENT ROOM AT SHAW HILL, CHORLEY, IN THE COUNTY OF LANCASTER.

COMPILED BY

R. D. RADCLIFFE,

M.A., CH. CH. OXFORD, F.S.A.,

HON. SEC. HISTORIC SOCIETY OF LANCASHIRE AND CHESHIRE.

———

PRIVATELY PRINTED.

1895.

T. BRAKELL LTD., LIVERPOOL.

1368290

SCHEDULE OF DEEDS AND DOCUMENTS, THE PROPERTY OF COLONEL THOMAS RICHARD CROSSE, PRESERVED IN THE MUNIMENT ROOM AT SHAW HILL, CHORLEY, IN THE COUNTY OF LANCASTER.

No. 1.   Liverpool.

S.D. Grant from William Le Barun to Randal de La More of Leverpol of two Landas in the territory of Leverpool; one in Le Lendig-feld, extending in length from the Sea to the Moor, and between the Landas of Geoffrey fil. Agnes and Randal de la Mor; the other in Le Hethylondes in the Nethere Wendiges between the Landas of Geoffrey fil. Scyas and Dawe del Bonke, rendering One Rose yearly at the Feast of St. John Baptist. The grantor's half burgage in Le Bonkestrete, in which he lived, to acquit the said Landas of all dues. Witnesses:

Thomas Faber, Ralph de Hybernia, William Balle, Richard Barun, William fil. Richard, John fil. Randal, and many others.

Vesica-shaped seal of green wax, impressed with a fleur-de-lis like ornament, surrounded by the legend [S]. WILLI . LE . BARVN.

No. 2.   Liverpool.

S.D. Grant from John del Mor of Lyverpol to Agnes, formerly wife of Randal de la Mor, his mother, of a Selion of land in the field del Hethylondes between the selions of Thomas fil. Brun and John fil. Simon, and of another selion of land in Le Wit-acres between the selions of John del Mor and Richard fil. Robert:

B

rendering yearly one obolus at the Nativity of our Lord. Witnesses :

John fil. Gernet, Ralph de Hibernia, Thomas Faber, Richard fil. Robert, William Balle, Geoffrey fil. Seyene, and others.

No. 3.   Liverpool.

s.d. Grant from Thomas fil. Brun to John le Poter and his heirs and assigns of a Selion of land in the territory of Lyverpol situate in Everstan between land of Roger Carpenter on the North and land of Alan Walsemon on the South extending in length from Everstan-dale to the little road in Le Hethilondes : rendering yearly one silver obolus at the Nativity of St. John Baptist. And a burgage lying in Le Dale strete between the tenements of Adam fil. Richard and Anable fil. William Balle will acquit the said selion of all dues to the chief lord of the fee. Witnesses :

John de la Mor, Alan Walsemon, Adam fil. Richard, William de Alkmundebery, Richard de la Mor, Richard fil. Richard, and many others.

Vesica-shaped seal of green wax, impressed with a fleur-de-lis of rude design, surrounded by a legend of which the name BRVN is alone decipherable.

No. 4.   Walton.

s.d. Grant from Richard lord of Walton to Peter Scissor and his heirs or assigns, or to whomsoever he wishes to bequeath or assign it, except men in Religion and Jews, of one Meadow in the territory of Walton, within the dyke, beginning and going lengthways from the dyke in the North West to a certain dyke in the South East, and lying between the land of John fil. Margery and the Huth-lone which leads to Derby wood : To hold of the grantor and his heirs by homage and free service with common of turbary, pasture, and other easements to the town of Walton belonging : rendering yearly to the grantor and his heirs one silver penny at the Feast of St. Michael for ever. Witnesses :

Robert le Burun, William de Ayntre, Robert de Kyrkdale, Henry de Acres, William the clerk, Richard de Blakemore, and many others.

Seal of white wax, illegible.

No. 5.   Lathum.

s.d. Grant from Robert fil. Robert de Lathum to John fil. Henry and Alice his wife and their joint heirs, and in

default of such heirs to the right heirs of John for
ever, of six acres and a half of land in Lathum, situate
in two places in Wolle-mor-side, of which one lies
between a certain enclosure of John de le Marclon and
the road, and the other between the land of Mandre
and the high way on the East side, together with
common of pasture, and all free liberties, customs, and
easements to the vill of Lathum appertaining : rendering yearly twelve silver pence at the Annunciation of
the Blessed Mary and the Feast of St. Michael, and a
payment of half a mark of silver on the death of his
father. Witnesses :

Alan Norreus, John Walens, Gilbert of the lordship
of Halsale, Ralph de Bikerstat, Richard Walens, and
others.

No. 6. *Wigan.*

s.d. Grant from Henry de Hastelegh, clerk, to Hugh de
Hastelegh, clerk, of a toft situate in the town of Wygan,
on the road which leads to the cowhouse of the lord
Rector of the Church of Wygan, between the burgages
of William Botlig's and Thomas de Eccleston, rendering
yearly to the lord of the town of Wygan the services
thence due and accustomed. Witnesses :

John de Cruce, John fil. Hugh, John de Birkehenede,
John le fferour, Henry fil. Holl, and others.

No. 7. *Wigan.*

s.d. Grant from William fil. William del Sedhevyd to Adam de
la Croz of a certain part of his land in the town of
Wygan, called Le Haly Welle Kar ; rendering yearly
three grains of pepper to the grantor and his heirs,
and four pence of customary money to the lord
of Wygan, for all services, to be paid on the accustomed quarter days. Witnesses :

Roger le Swyneleys, Hugh de Bullyng, Hugh
Mercenarius, Walter le Walker, Adam le Cnyf-smyt,
William the clerk, and others.

Oval seal of green wax, with cruciform ornament in
the centre, surrounded by the legend s . WILLI . DE .
SEDHEVID.

No. 8. *Liverpool.*

s.d. Grant from Ranulfe fil. Thomas Faber of Lyverpol to
Richard fil. John fil. Symon and his heirs or assigns of
a Selion of land in the territory of Lyverpol, situate in
Le Dale feld, between land of the grantor on the South

side and land of Adam de Wolveton on the North side, together with the fourth part of a Burgage, part of the grantor's one and a half acres lying in Le Hethylondes between the grantor's land on one side and land of Marjorie wife of Ralph de Hybernia on the other side : rendering yearly three silver pence to the chief lord, and to the grantor and his heirs one silver obolus. Witnesses :

John de Mora, Alan Walsemon, Adam fil. Richard, Richard fil. Richard, William fil. Ralph, and others.

No. 9. *Solihull.*

s.d. Grant by John de Blinshue-Wyk of Sulihull, in free alms for his soul, the soul of Dionysia his wife, and the souls of their ancestors and descendants, of a yearly rent of eight pence for the support of a Lamp before the Altar and in honour of the Blessed Mary, in the church at Sulihull, which rent Alexander de Brockhurst and his heirs paid the grantor for a certain tenement held by them of him in his manor of Brockhurst, and lying between the moor of Brockhurst and land of the said Alexander. Witnesses :

Walter de Winterton, William de Melton, Thomas Sulqui de Longedon, Henry Le Barun de la Coppe, Robert de la Coppe, and others.

No. 10. *Berkeswelle.*

s.d. Release and quitclaim from Gilbert de Kenteil of Warewick to Sir Richard de Amundeville and his heirs, of all right and claim the grantor had in Richard Barri and in his goods, land, and services within the territory of Berkeswelle. Witnesses :

Sir Henry Harãg, Simon the Chaplain, Ralph de Anet, William de Lamare, Gerard de St. Licio, Walter de Morcote, Philip de Berkeswelle, John de Oldenhale, Walter le Newcome, Jordan le Stalwarde chaplain, Henry Barri, Nigel fil. Hugh, and many others.

Ancient transcript on parchment of three following deeds [viz., Nos. 11 a, 11 b, 11 c].

No. 11 a. *Pemberton.*

1293. Grant from Simon fil. Thurstan de Holond to William fil. Roger de Ines, dwelling in Pemberton, and his heirs or assigns, of a Messuage and Bovate of land in Pemberton, which the grantor had of the feoffment of Henry de Tildislegh, and of which he enfeoffed William son of Adam de Pemberton. Witnesses :

Adam de Pemberton, Henry de Pemberton, William de Winstanislegh, Roger de Winstanislegh, Henry de Winstanislegh, John de Cruce, John Dun, Matthew the clerk, and others.

Given at Wygan on Wednesday next after the Feast of All Saints [4th Nov.], 1293.

NO. 11 B. *Pemberton.*

1293. Release and quitclaim from Simon de Holond to William fil. Roger de Ines, dwelling in Pemberton, and his heirs, of all right and claim in a certain messuage and one bovate of land in the town of Pemberton, called Le Tounsted, of which the grantor had been enfeoffed by Henry de Tildislegh, and which lands Cristiana de Radclive formerly held. Witnesses :

Adam lord of Pemberton, Henry fil. Roger de Winstanislegh, William de Winstanislegh, Adam de Orel, Robert fil. Sir Robert de Holond, John de Cruce, Henry the clerk, and others.

Given at Wygan on Wednesday next after All Saints' Day [4th Nov.], 1293.

NO. 11 C. *Pemberton.*

S.D. Grant from William de Pemberton to Cristiana daughter of Adam de Radclif, of one bovate of land in the town of Pemberton, called Le Tounstede, which Aynhou de Pemberton held of the grantor : rendering fifteen pence and a halfpenny of silver yearly by four payments, namely, at Christmas four pence, at the Annunciation four pence, at the Feast of St. John Baptist four pence, and at the Feast of St. Michael three pence and a halfpenny. Witnesses :

Sir Robert de Lathum then Sheriff of Lancashire, Sir Robert de Holond, Peter de Burnul, Hugh de Haidoc, Thurstan de Holond then Bailiff of Makerfeld, Jordan Kenian, and others.

NO. 12. *Wigan.*

1293. Grant from Richard le Walker of Wygan to Thomas fil. Roger the chief carpenter of Wygan of half a Toft of land in the town of Wygan, lying near the lane which leads from Bateystegele to the old mill, of which one end abuts on the high road and the other on Dog clif: To be held of the lord of Wygan and his successors, rendering yearly to the said lord six silver pennies by four quarterly payments at the accustomed times. Witnesses :

Mathew de Modburleye, Walter the fuller, William de Frekilton, Adam fil. Richard, Roger fil. Richard, Richard Page, Nicholas the clerk, and others.

Given at Wygan, on Tuesday next after the Feast of St. Hillary, 22 Edward I. [19th Jan., 1293].

Small oval seal of green wax, on which is a squirrel, surrounded by a legend.

No. 13. *Wigan.*

s.d.   Grant from Adam de Cruce to Elene his daughter, of a plot of land in the town of Wygan, called Le Rie field, and a plot of land called Le Hali walle Kar, and the half toft which he had of the gift of Hugh de Haydoc, lying between the toft of William Eldware and the half toft of Adam le Couper ; rendering three grains of pepper yearly to the grantor and his heirs, and to the chief lord of the town of Wigan, sixteen pence, by four payments at the accustomed times of year, for all services. Witnesses :

Roger de Swyneley, John de Birkehened, Adam de Swyneley, Adam fil. Richard de Marclan, Henry de Muckelfen, Nicholas the clerk, and others.

No. 14. *Wigan.*

1299.   Release and quitclaim from John de Cruce de Wigan to Alan fil. Walter the fuller and his heirs by Elene his wife, sister of the grantor, all his right and claim in all the land in the town of Wigan which the said Alan took in free marriage with the said Elene, that is to say, in a half toft and house lying between the toft of William Oldware and the toft of Adam de Byrchene-schaye, in a certain plot of land called Le Ruy feld, lying between land of William del Stetheved and land of Nicholas de Tildesleye, and in a certain plot called Hali walle Karr, between the land of Nicholas de Tildesleye and the water of Dogles. Witnesses :

John de Birkehened, Robert de Roghinton, Roger de Leylond, John fil. Hugh the mercer, William fil. Walter, and others.

Given at Wigan, on Tuesday next after the Feast of St. Michael, " in monte tumba," 27 Edw. I. [1299].

No. 14*. *Wigan.*

1304. Grant from Roger fil. William fil. Hulle of Wygan, to John de Cruce and his heirs and assigns, of all land which the grantor had in Le Struyndes in the islands of Wygan, lying on the east side of the high road which leads from the town of Wygan towards Out-towne Bridge ; To be held of the lord of the town of Wygan by the services due and accustomed. Witnesses :

William de Brade[shaw], Richard de Ines, Henry de Ines, Richard de fful[shagh], John de Byrkehened, John fil. Hugh the mercer, Alan the fuller and others.

Given at Wygan on Monday next after the Feast of St. Luke the Evangelist [19th October], 1304.

No. 15. *Wigan.*

1305. Power of attorney from Hugh de Standish to Robert le Pierpoint to deliver seisin to Richard de Pilkington and his heirs and assigns of all lands and tenements which he the said Hugh de Standish had of the feoffment of Adam de Asshagh. Given at Wygan on Monday next after the Feast of St. Leonard, 33 Edw. I. [8 Nov. 1305].

No. 16. *Liverpool.*

1305. Grant from Adam fil. Ranulph of Lyverpol to Richard de Mapeldurem and his heirs or assigns of two Bovates of land lying in the field called Le Dale feld, next the king's highway on one side and the land of Robert de Merser on the other, to be held of the chief lords of the fee. And the grantor's burgage in Le Mor strete between the tenements of Roger fil. Ewenild and John de Mora will acquit the said bovates of all dues to the chief lords. Witnesses :

John de Mora, Alan Walsemon, William Boron, John Poter, Richard de Mora, and others.

Given at Lyverpol on the Feast of St. Gregory the Pope [12th March], 1305.

No. 17. *Wigan.*

1308. Release and quitclaim from Thomas fil. Alan the plumber to William fil. Walter the fuller of Wygan his heirs and assigns of all land and buildings in the town of Wygan which the grantor had of the feoffment of Robert de Rovynton, lying between the toft of Emme de Rovynton on one side and the house of the grantee on the other. Witnesses :

William de Brades[haigh], Richard de Ines, John de Cruce, John de Byrkehened, Robert de Rovynton, Alan the fuller, Hugh the clerk, and others.

Given at Wygan on Tuesday in the week of Pentecost [4th June] 1308.

No. 18. *Liverpool.*

1309. Grant from William fil. Robert de Aynolfisdale to William fil. Richard de Aynolfisdale of a fourth part of a Burgage in the town of Levirpole, lying between land of Richard de Rome on the one side and land of Robert fil. Agnes on the other side, in Le Walle feld, rendering yearly to the chief lord of the fee three silver pennies, namely, at the Feast of St. Michael the Archangel one penny and a halfpenny, and at the Annunciation of the Blessed Virgin Mary one penny and a halfpenny, for all services. Witnesses:

John de Mora, Adam the clerk, then bailiffs, Adam fil. William, Robert fil. Hanne, Adam Baroun, and others.

Given at Leverpole 5th April, 3 Edw. II. [1309].

No. 19. *Wigan.*

1310. Release and quitclaim from William fil. William de Preston and Elyanore daughter of Nicholas de Wygan, clerk, to John de la Croyz of Wygan his heirs and assigns, of all the grantor's right and claim in eight acres of land in the town and territory of Wygan and in half of Henne hurste meadow in the same town, which eight acres and three acres, with buildings, lie abutting lengthways, at one end, upon the toft of William Russel and Richard fil. Michael, and at the other end, upon Le Stanygate, leading from Wygan towards Pemberton, and are bounded on one side by land of Richard fil. Adam fil. Ormi in the North, and on the other, the South side, by the half acre which William de Preston sold to Mathew [the] clerk; one acre of land called Hitchefeld, and one acre known as Le Lorimeres acre; and two half acres, one called Le Hengande half acre, and the other called Le Lomy half acre; and two acres lying on the north side of the high road leading from Wygan to Pemberton, which two acres William Russel the elder had of the gift of John de la Croyz. Witnesses:

Sir William de Holand, knight, William de Bradeshaghe, Richard de Ines, Adam de Pemberton, Master

Richard de ffuleshaghe, John fil. Hugh, Roger de Lever, Hugh the clerk, and others.

Given at Wygan on Monday in the Feast of St. Bartholomew the Apostle, 4 Edw. II. [31st Aug. 1310].

No. 20. *Wigan.*

1311. Grant from Gilbert fil. Gilbert de Wyk to Edmund fil. Jordan de Stanedissh of a toft in the town and territory of Wygan, lying between the toft of the grantee which he had of the feoffment of Adam de Halifax, and the toft of Adam fil. Richard de la Croyz, to be held of the lord of the town of Wygan by the services accustomed. Witnesses :

William de Stanedissh, Master Richard de ffulshagh, John de la Croyz, John fil. Hugh, Roger de Lever, Henry de ffulshaghe, Hugh the clerk, and others.

Given at Wygan on Friday the Vigil of the Nativity [24th Dec.], 1311.

Six-sided seal of green wax, impressed with a frog, surrounded by an illegible inscription.

No. 21. *Wigan.*

1311. Grant from Henry fil. Hugh de Wygan to Adam de Cophull his heirs and assigns of a toft in the town and territory of Wygan, which Adam Cambayn formerly held of the grantor, lying in Le Hallegate next the toft of Master Richard de ffulshaghe, to be held of the lord of the town of Wygan by the services accustomed. Witnesses :

Master Richard de ffulshaghe, John de la Croyz, John de Byrkehened, John fil. Hugh, Roger de Lever, William fil. Walter, William de Rovynton, Hugh the clerk, and others.

Given at Wygan on Monday next after the Feast of St. Hillary the Bishop [18th Jan.], 1311.

Round seal of green wax, showing a cormorant looking to the right, surrounded by an illegible inscription.

No. 22. *Wigan.*

1313. Deed of gift from Adam fil. Robert Carpenter of Wygan to Thomas his son of all his goods and chattels, moveable and immoveable, above and below the ground, within and without his houses, in all the land and buildings belonging to him in the town of Wygan. Witnesses :

John de la Croyz, John de Byrkehened, John fil. Hugh, Roger de Lever, Thomas fil. Richard, Henry de Marclan, Hugh the clerk, and others.

Given at Wygan on Friday next after the Feast of the Circumcision [5th January], 1313.

No. 23 A.   *Wigan.*

S.D.   Grant from John de Birkehenyd to Adam fil. Robert Carpenter and Richard fil. Michael of Wygan and their heirs of a toft and one acre of land in the town of Wygan, as the grantor received them from the lord of the town of Wygan, and which lie between Longe leye and the land of Roger de Swinleye ; rendering yearly one obolus of silver to the grantor and his heirs on All Saints Day, and to the lord of Wygan twelve pence by four quarterly payments on the accustomed days. Witnesses :

Adam fil. Orm, William fil. Hulle, Henry Faber, Richard Carpenter, Hugh fil. Roger, William the clerk, and others.

No. 23 B.   *Wigan.*

S.D.   Grant from Richard fil. Michael of Wygan to Adam fil. Robert Carpenter and his heirs of a half toft and one acre of land in the town of Wygan, which he had of John de Birkehened ; Rendering yearly to the grantor and his heirs on St. John Baptist's Day a Rose, and to the lord of Wygan six silver pennies at the accustomed times. Witnesses :

Master Richard de ffulshahe the "Senescall," John de Birkehened, Hugh the mercer, Robert de Rovinton, Thomas fil. Adam, Thomas fil. Roger, Richard the clerk, and others.

No. 23 C.   *Wigan.*

S.D.   Grant from Thomas fil. Roger the chief carpenter of Wygan to Adam fil. Robert the carpenter of Wygan in free marriage with Mariota the grantor's sister, and their joint heirs, of the fourth part of all the land which he had of Master Adam de Waleton, then Rector of the church of Wygan, bounded lengthways on one side by land of Roger de Swinleye, on the other by the road which leads from the house formerly Thomas Page's to Staned[ish], and lying between lands of Hugh Mercer, John de Birkehenyd, and John Baker ; Rendering yearly to the grantor and his heirs on Christmas Day a barbed arrow of iron, and to the lord of the town of

Wygan six pence of silver by four quarterly payments on the accustomed days. Witnesses :

Roger de Swinleye, Hugh Mercer, Hugh de Bullyng, John de Birkehenyd, William fil. Hulle, William fil. Orm, Henry Faber, and others.

Oval seal of green wax, showing a tuft of iris leaves surrounded by the legend—S . THOME . FIL . ROG .

No. 23 D. *Liverpool.*

1315. Grant from John de Kyrkeby to Adam de Cholale and his heirs or assigns of a plot of land with buildings thereon, which the grantor had of Adam fil. Richard, in the town of Liverpoll, situate in Le Castel stret, between the grantor's own tenement on the north side and the tenement formerly of Adam fil. Richard on the south side, which plot is at the top next the road, twenty four feet wide, in the middle sixteen feet, and in length sixty five feet ; Rendering yearly to the chief lord of the fee four pence and one obolus of silver, in equal portions, at the Feasts of St. Michael the Archangel and the Annunciation ; also rendering to John fil. William nine silver pennies, in equal portions, at Christmas Day and the Nativity of St. John Baptist ; also rendering to Richard le Somenour and his heirs four pence and one obolus of silver, in equal portions, at the Feasts of St. Michael and all Angels and the Annunciation ; also rendering to the heirs of Roger de Sonky one silver obolus at the Feast of St. Martin in winter. Witnesses :

John de Mora, Richard de Mora, William fil. Radulph, William de Kirkedale, William Walchemon, and others.

Given at Liverpoll on Sunday next before the Feast of St. Mark the Evangelist, 8 Edw. II. [20th April, 1315].

No. 23 E. *Wigan.*

1315. Indenture made between John de Cruce of the one part and Alan the fuller of Wygan of the other part. Reciting that contentions and controversies had arisen between the parties hereto, in consequence of which the said John had impleaded the said Alan and Elene his wife on account of certain tenements in Wygan : And that the said Alan had impleaded the said John in respect of certain sums of money, part of the settlement made on the marriage of the said Alan with the said Elene : It was then agreed between the parties :—

That the said John should release to Alan and Elene
and their heirs all his claim to the said tenements ;
And that Alan and Elene should release all their claims
against John in respect of the said marriage settlement ;
Mutual Bonds to be signed by the parties hereto, and
kept in the custody of John de Byrkehened. Witnesses :

Richard de Ines, John Gyllybrond, Adam de Hynde-
legh, Roger de Lever, Nicholas de Cruce, Hugh the
clerk, and others.

Given at Wygan on Wednesday next after Sunday on
which "Quasi modo geniti" is sung [2nd April],
8 Edw. II. [1315].   Seal gone.

No. 24.   *Liverpool.*

1315. Grant from Richard Prendirgest of Liverpoll to Adam fil.
William fil. Radulph of a selion of land in the territory
of Liverpoll, lying in le Chirhes-accris, between the
tenement of Elene Baron on one side, and the tenement of Alan fil. John.   And the heirs of William de
Castello will acquit the said selion against the chief
lord of the fee.   Witnesses :

John de la Mor, Richard de la Mor, William ffox,
William Walchemon, Richard Baron, and others.

Given at Liverpoll on the Vigil of St. Bartholomew,
9 Edw. II. [23rd Aug., 1315].

No. 25.   *Wigan.*

1316. Grant from Richard de Ines to Almaric the fuller of
Wygan and his lawful heirs of a certain plot of land
with buildings in the town of Wygan, lying between the
dwelling house of William the leather dresser and the
dwelling house of William fil. Neel ; Rendering yearly
to the grantor and his heirs two shillings and sixpence
of silver to be paid in equal portions according to the
custom of the town of Wygan : In default of such issue
of the grantee, remainder to the grantor and his heirs.
Witnesses :

John de Cruce, John de Byrkehenede, John fil. Hugh,
Alan fil. Walter, William fil. Walter, Robert del Heghefeld, William Botlinge, Hugh the clerk, and others.

Given at Wygan on Wednesday in the Feast of St.
Dunstan the Archbishop [26th May], 1316.

No. 26.   *Wigan.*

1316. Release and quitclaim from Amota, who was the wife of
Stephen Hanne knave of Wygan, in her pure widowhood,
to Richard del Stanistrete, of her right and claim, by

way of dower, in half a toft and buildings in Le Mulne-
gate in the town of Wygan, which the said Richard had
of the feoffment of Stephen Hanne knave. Witnesses :
Gilbert de Culchith, John de Cruce, John fil. Hugh,
Robert del Heghefeld, Hugh de Hagh, William de
Rovinton, William fil. William "curatoris," the clèrk,
and others.

Given at Wygan on Monday next after the Feast of
the Holy Trinity [7th June], 1316.

No. 27.   *Wigan.*

1316. Grant from Eadmund de Stanedissh to Almaric the fuller
of Wygan and his heirs and assigns of a toft in
Wygan, lying between a toft which the grantor had of
the gift of Gilbert de Wyk on one side, and a certain
narrow lane leading towards Le Coppe de Hal Mulne
on the other side, one end of which extends to the
land of Nicholas de Tyldesleghe, and the other to the
high road leading from Wygan to Stanedissh : To be
held of the lord of Wygan by the services due and
accustomed. Witnesses :
John de Cruce, John de Byrkehened, John fil. Hugh,
Alan the fuller, William de Rovynton, William fil. . . .
Hugh the clerk, and others.

Given at Wygan on Monday next after the Feast of
the Assumption of the Blessed Virgin Mary [16th
Aug.], 1316.

No. 28.   *Liverpool.*

1316. Lease whereby Richard fil. Adam de Liverpoll demises
and to farm lets to Adam fil. William fil. Ralph, one
Selion of land in the territory of Liverpoll lying in le
quit halkris [white acres] between the tenement of
Adam Balle on one side and the tenement of Alexander
fil. Masse de Walay on the other side, for the term of
three full years, from the Feast of St. Michael the Archangel, 10 Edw. II.; but for which lease and delivery
the said Adam has lent to Richard for the said term
in hand twenty shillings of silver, so that the said
Richard or his heirs should pay the money at the
end of the term aforesaid. And if it should happen
that the said selion shall have to be sold or disposed
of during the aforesaid term, Adam shall have the
preference before all others at the price of twelve pence.
It is also agreed that the said Adam shall retain the said
selion in his hands until the said debt shall be paid in
full. Witnesses :

John de Mora, Richard de Mora, William ffox, Richard Baroun, Richard de Southsex, and others.

Given at Liverpoll on Sunday next before the Feast of St. Michael the Archangel in the year above named [26th Sept. 1316].

No. 29.   *Wigan.*

1317. Grant from Richard Page of Wygan to John de Cruce of Wygan his heirs and assigns of a certain part of his land in the town of Wygan, three feet in width beyond the house of the said John, and extending from the high road to the garden pertaining to the grantor's dwelling house, so that it should have a breadth of three feet beyond the posts of the said John's house : To hold of the lord of the town of Wygan by the accustomed services. Witnesses :

Richard de Ines, John de Byrkehened, John fil. Hugh, William fil. Walter, Henry de ffulshaghe, William de Rovynton, Hugh Mareschall, William fil. William the dyer, Hugh the clerk, and others.

Given at Wygan on Tuesday next before the Feast of St. Gregory the Martyr [28th Sept.], 1316.

Heater-shaped seal of green wax, bearing a bird perched on a branch, on a chief a roundle between two letters, LL.

No. 30.   *Wigan.*

1317. Grant in fee farm from John de Cruce of Wygan to Adam fil. John the baker of a plot of land in Wygan lying between the toft of John le fferour and the toft of the grantee, upon which his bakehouse is built ; rendering yearly four pence of silver to the grantor and his heirs by equal payments at Christmas and the Nativity of St. John Baptist. Witnesses :

Richard de Ines, Henry de ffulshaghe, John fil. Hugh, Henry Russel, William fil. Walter, Hugh the dyer, Hugh the clerk, and others.

Given at Wygan on Sunday in the octave of the Circumcision [2nd Jan.], 1317.

No. 31.   *Liverpool.*

1318. Grant from Aldous fil. Elot del Hout-lone to William . . . . . del Balchagh of half a burgage in the town of Liverpoll, situate in Le Dale-feld, between the tenement of Andrew fil. Mathew and the tenement of Adam fil. Thomas Brouneson : To be held of the chief lords of the fee by the accustomed services. Witnesses :

John de Mora, Richard de Mora, Richard Southsex, Robert fil. Hugh, Robert fil. Henry, Richard fil. Richard, Adam fil. William, and many others.

Given at Liverpoll 19th December, 12 Edw. II. [1318].

No. 32.   *Wigan.*

1319. Release from Emme, who was the wife of John Baker of Wygan, to Adam fil. Robert Carpenter of Wygan, and Thomas his son and their heirs, of all right and claim which she had by way of Dower in the land in Wygan, which the said Adam had of the feoffment of the said John her late husband. Witnesses :

John de Cruce, John de Byrkchened, John fil. Hugh, Henry de ffulschagh, Robert del Heghefeld, Hugh the clerk, and others.

Given at Wygan on Friday the morrow of Saint Peter in Cathedra [23rd Feb.], 1319.

No. 33.   *Liverpool.*

1319. Grant from Alice de Altekar, in exercise of her lawful right and being of sound mind, to her eldest son John of a plot of land in the town of Liverpoll, with a house and curtilage, situate in Le Dale strete, between the tenement of Richard Trewe and the tenement of Mathew fil. Richard; and half an acre of meadow land in Le Wallefeld, between the tenement of Richard Mapleduram and the garden of John de Aynolisdale, which plots came to her by inheritance from her brother Adam : To be held of the chief lord of the fee by the accustomed services. On failure of John's legitimate heirs the property to revert to the right heirs of the grantor. Witnesses :

John de Mora, Richard de Mora, Richard de Southsex, Robert fil. Henry, Richard fil. Richard, Adam fil. William, and others.

Given at Liverpoll on Tuesday next after Easter [10th April], 12 Edw. II. [1319].

No. 34.   *Wigan.*

1323. Grant from Agnes, who was the wife of Henry le Boghe Wryghte of Wygan, in pure widowhood, to Thomas fil. Adam fil. Robert Carpenter of Wygan and Alice her daughter and their lawful issue for the term of the grantor's life, of an acre of land in Wygan, situate next the grantor's own land, of which one end extends to the land of Roger the merchant and the

other to the high road which leads from Wygan to
Shevynton. After the death of the said Agnes the pro-
perty to revert to the grantor and her heirs. Witnesses :
John de Cruce, John fil. Hugh, John de Byrkehened,
Henry de ffulshaghe, Mathew de Marclan, Henry de
Marclan, Hugh the clerk, and others.

Given at Wygan on Monday next after the Feast of
St. Hillary the Bishop [17th Jan.], 1323.

No. 35.   *Wigan.*

1323. Grant from Almaric the fuller of Wygan to Roger le
Mercer of Stanedish his heirs and assigns of half a burgage and buildings in the town of Wygan, situate
between the burgage of Thomas Tannar and the half
burgage of the said Roger ; Rendering to the lord of the
town of Wygan the services due and accustomed, and
to Thomas Tannar and his heirs yearly two shillings in
silver at the Feast of St. Margaret the Virgin. Witnesses :
William de Stanedish, Thomas de Longetre, John de
Cruce, John fil. Hugh, Henry de ffulshaghe, William
Botling, Alan the fuller, Hugh the clerk, and others.

Given at Wygan on Monday next after the Feast of
St. Scolastica the Virgin [14th Feb.], 1323.

No. 36.   *Wigan.*

1324. Grant from John de Cruce of Wygan to Thurstan his son
and the heirs of his body lawfully begotten of a certain
part of his lands and tenements in Wygan, to wit, that
burgage upon which the grantor's capital messuage is
built, between the burgage of Richard Burgeys and the
burgage of John del Marsh ; also one burgage with a
messuage which the grantor had by the demise of Margery
his sister ; and the Greater Hey called Le Ei-clyves ;
and a plot of land called Hytchefeld ; and Le Longefeld.
and an acre of land next Le Stanrygate, which was formerly Hugh de Haghe's, with a great barn built on it ;
and a plot of land called Hanna-hurste medowe ; and
a plot of ground called Le Hengan-dich-half-acre ; and
a plot of ground called Lomy-half-acre ; and all the
grantor's land in Le Quereyes ; together with the reversion to all land which Emme Russell held in dower in
that plot : To hold to the said Thurstan and the heirs
of his body lawfully begotten ; with successive remain-
ders in tail male to his son William, and to his daughter
Matilda by her husband Henry Banastre. Witnesses :

Richard de Ines, Adam de Pemberton, Gilbert de Culchyth, Henry de Pemberton, Roger de Wynstancesleghe, John fll. Hugh, Henry de ffulshaghe, William fil. Walter, William the dyer, clerk, and others.

Given at Wygan on Sunday in the octave of St. Hillary the Bishop [14tn Jan.], 1324.

Small oval seal of green wax, with a stag's head and neck, surrounded by an inscription.

No. 37. *Wigan.*

1325. Grant from Thurstan fil. John de Cruce of Wygan to John de Cruce, his father, for the term of his natural life, of all the messuages lands and tenements which the said Thurstan had of the gift of the said John, except a messuage and curtilage which Agnes Hornby held for a term of years, and except six acres of land lying in Wygan heghes, called the Lomy halvacre and the Hengande halv acre, and except five acres of land lying next these, and except the third part of a certain heye called Le Eclives ; Rendering a Rose yearly at the Nativity of St. John Baptist to the grantor and his heirs, and to the chief lord of the town of Wygan the services due and accustomed. Witnesses :

Richard de Ines, Adam de Pemberton, John de Chysenhale, William Gilibrond, John fil. Hugh, Henry de ffulshagh, Richard the clerk, and others.

Given at Wygan on St. Margaret's day [20th July], 19 Edw. II. [1325].

No. 38. *Wigan.*

1325. Grant from Adam de Layland to Matilda his daughter and her heirs by Roger Stanedish her husband, of one half burgage with buildings, situate in Wygan between the burgage of William fil. Walter and another half burgage of the grantor. To be held of the lord of the town of Wygan by the accustomed services. In default reversion to the grantor and his heirs. Witnesses :

Richard de Ines, William de Stanedish, John de Cruce, John fil. Hugh, Henry de ffulshaghe, William fil. Walter, William Botling, Hugh the clerk, and others.

Given at Wygan on Friday in the octave of St. Lucy the Virgin [20th Dec.], 1325.

No. 39. *Liverpool.*

1310. Grant from William Baron to Adam fil. William fil. Ralph and his heirs and assigns of three selions of land in

C

Lyverpul, bounded by a tenement of Henry de Wolvis-hegh on the North and by a tenement of Adam de Mareschal on the South, one end abutting on the road from the Hethilonds and the other on Everston-dale : To be held of the chief lords of the fee.   And three parts of a burgage in the Mor-croftis, between the land of Robert fil. Hugh and land of William de Mor, will acquit these selions from the chief lord.   Witnesses :

John de Mor, Richard de Mor, William Walschemō, Richard fil. Richard, John the clerk, and others.

Given at Lythirpul on Tuesday in Easter week [21st April], 3 Edw. II. [1310].

No. 40.   *Liverpool.*

1323. Grant from Robert fil. Henry de Lyverpoll to William his son and Alice his daughter jointly and to their heirs or assigns of half an acre of land, one third part thereof excepted, in the territory of the aforesaid town of Lyverpoll, lying in Les Hethilondes, between land of William Fox on one side and land of Roger de Carnarvan on the other, which the grantor had of the feoffment of Richard de Ruy'ton : To be held of the chief lord of the fee : In case one of the grantees should die without lawful heirs the whole of the land to go to the other. Witnesses :

John de Mora, Richard de Mora, Richard de Southsex, Adam the clerk, Adam Baron, and others.

Given at Lyverpoll on Monday next after the Feast of the Translation of Thomas the Martyr [11th July], 19 Edw. II. [1323].

No. 41.   *Wigan.*

1324. Grant from John fil. Walter the fuller of Wygan to Almaric the fuller of Wygan his heirs and assigns of all his arable land lying in a certain plot called Habbeheleghe, between land of Alice de Clayton and land neither ploughed nor broken up, which the grantor and the said Alice held, enclosed and unenclosed, one end of which said land extends to Swynleghe-heye and the other to the Out-lone which leads from that land to the high road from Wygan to Stanedissh : To be held of the lord of the town of Wygan by the accustomed services.   Witnesses :

Richard de Ines, John de Cruce, John de Byrkehened, Henry de ffulshagh, William fil. Walter, William Botling, Hugh the clerk, and others.

Given at Wygan on Thursday in the octave of St. Valentine the Martyr [15th Feb.], 1324.

No. 42.   *Liverpool.*

1329. Grant from Cecilia, who was the wife of Adam de Utting, in her pure widowhood, to Richard de Walton of one half burgage in the town of Lyverpull, situate in Le Dale strete between the tenement of William Baret on the east and the tenement of Richard Tewe on the west : To be held of the chief lords of the fee, rendering yearly to Alexander son of Mathew de Waley and his heirs eighteen silver pennies, in equal portions at the Feast of St. Michael, the Purification, and the Nativity of St. John Baptist. Witnesses :

John de Mora, Richard de Mora, Adam fil. William, Adam the clerk, Adam Baroun, and others.

Given at Lyverpull, 14th April, 3 Edw. III. [1329].

No. 43.   *Wigan.*

1333. Grant from Robert fil. William de Bolton to Robert fil. Sir Thomas de Burnhull clerk of all his goods and chattels, moveable and immoveable, lying on a certain plot of land, with the buildings thereon, which the grantor had given the said Robert by deed. Witnesses :

Richard de Ines, Henry de ffulschagh, John fil. Hugh, Symon Payn, William fil. Walter, William the dyer, Henry Gilibrond, and others.

Given at Wygan on Friday next after the Feast of St. Mark the Evangelist [30th April], 1333.

Small round seal of brown wax, showing, among foliage, a squirrel, a rabbit, and a dog [?], inscribed in Gothic letters - - S PVRSOVIE - - RI -

No. 44.   *Wigan.*

1333. Grant from Richard Botling to Master Robert de Burnull of all his property, growing and not growing, moveable and immoveable, which he had in one half toft with its appurtenances, in the town of Wygan. Given at Wygan on Sunday in the Feast of St. Mark the Evangelist [1st May], 1333. No witnesses.

No. 45.   *Wigan.*

1334. Grant from Henry Russel, the elder, of Wygan to John fil. Richard fil. Dobbe of Wygan his heirs and assigns of one acre of land in the town of Wygan, between the grantor's land on one side and the grantee's land on the other, one end of which extends to the water of Dogles and the other to Le Stanrygate ; To hold of the lord of the town of Wygan and his successors by the services accustomed. Witnesses :

Gilbert de Ines, John fil. Hugh, Henry de ffulschagh, Symon Payn, William fil. Walter, William the dyer, Walter the clerk, and others.

Given at Wygan on Thursday next after the Feast of St. Ambrose [7th April], 1334.

Seal broken, but the letters . . . . STAN.* may be made out.

No. 46.   *Heath Charnock.*

1282. Release and quitclaim from Alice, formerly the wife of William fil. Margaret, and Richard her son and heir, to Ralph fil. William Gogard his heirs and assigns, of all their right and claim in a certain plot of land with appurtenances in Het Chernock called Waltre-riddinges, which Adam fil. Thomas Gogard sold to the said Ralph. Witnesses :

William de Stand[ish], John de Copphul, John de Chyesenale, Robert of the same place, Adam del Hull, Robert the clerk, and others.

Given at Hetchernock on Wednesday next after the Assumption of the Blessed Virgin Mary [19th August], 10 Edw. I. [1282].

No. 47.   *Rivington.*

1338. Grant from William de Asshogh to William fil. Hugh de Asshogh and Richard his brother for their lives, of a certain plot of land in the town of Revynton called Yarwar ; rendering yearly for the first twenty years a silver penny at the Assumption of the Blessed Virgin Mary, afterwards one marc [?] of silver at the time appointed : In default the third part of the said land to revert to the grantor and his heirs. Witnesses :

John de Standish, William de Worthinton, William de Adlington, John de Cophull, Richard the clerk, and others.

Given at Wygan on Monday next after the Feast of St. Martin in winter [16th Nov.], 12 Edw. III. [1338].

No. 48.   *Liverpool.*

1338. Letter in Norman French from Henry Earl of Lancaster and Leicester, Seneschal of England, to William le Blount, Sheriff of Lancashire, as to payments to be made by the Earl's tenants at Liverpool on entering into possession of land. Given at Kenilworth 10th of Aug., in the 11th year of his Earldom [1338].

No. 49.   *Halewood.*

1339. Grant from Cecilia fil. John fil. Richard the Reeve of Crounton to Roger del Yate of Crounton his heirs and assigns of two acres of land in the territory of Halewode, lying next the Holebrok : To hold of the chief lord of the fee by the accustomed services, with common of pasture in Halewode. Witnesses :

John de Holand of Hale, John de Ditton, John de Dichefeld, Richard del Doustes, John de Grelle, Thomas fil. Stephen de Ditton, Richard de Alvandelegh, and others.

Given at Halewode on Monday next after the Feast of St. Peter ad Vincula [6th Aug.], 13 Edw. III. [1339].

No. 50.   *Walton.*

1339. Grant from Henry fil. Robert de ffasacreley to William fil. Richard fil. John his heirs and assigns of one acre of land which he had of the feoffment of Robert his father, lying in Le Heye, next the land of Richard fil. Richard de ffasacreley, and extending to the land of Richard le Harper de Longelegh, with liberty of ingress and egress to and from Le Belamys gate, following Le Old-erthe up to le Legh, and from le Legh up to the said acre ; To be held of the chief lord of the fee by the accustomed services for ever. Witnesses :

Symon fil. William de Walton, Henry de Atherton, William de Stonbriggelay, Adam de Irland, Thomas de Penereth, John de Accres, and others.

Given at Walton on Sunday next after the Feast of St. Edmund King and Martyr [21st Nov.], 13 Edw. III. [1339].

No. 51.   *Wigan.*

1340. Grant from John fil. Robert de Prestecot to Master Robert de Burnhull, his heirs and assigns, of one plot of land with buildings and appurtenances in the town of Wygan, situate in Standisshgate, between the land of Adam fil. John del Merssh, and land which the grantor had of Robert de Bolton ; Rendering a Rose yearly at the Nativity of St. John Baptist to Robert de Bolton and his heirs during the life of the grantor. Witnesses :

D

Adam de Pemberton, Henry de ffulshagh, Symon Payn, William le Lyster, Henry Gilibrond, William fil. Walter, Robert de Keucrdale clerk, and others.

Given at Wygan on Tuesday in the Octave of the Beheading of St. John Baptist [Aug. 29], 14 Edward III. [1340].

(Seal of green wax: a fleur-de-lis, and small hook between a pair of open shears, points upwards.)

No. 52.　　　*Charnock Richard.*

1344/5. Thomas fil. Thomas de Addilington to Robert de Derbyshire his heirs and assigns. Quit-claim to the reversion of a certain plot of land in the town of Charnok richart, together with three acres of land, appurtenances, buildings and gardens in the same town, which Roger Hitchcokson holds of the feoffment of William Hitchcokson. Witnesses:

John de Standissh, Henry de Charnok, Richard de Standissh, William de Worthington, John Nightgale, Thomas Weuer and others.

Given at Charnok on Tuesday in the Octave of Holy Innocents [4th Jan.], 18 Edward III. [1344/5].

No. 53.　　　*Flint.*

1346. Lease from Roger de Haregne of fflynt to Richard de Macclesfeld of half an acre of arable land in the territory of fflynt for a term of four years from Michaelmas 20 Edward III. at a rent of five shillings a year, the same to be renewed every four years for a like period provided the rent be punctually paid. Witnesses:

Richard del Hogh, then Mayor of the town of fflynt, Adam de Haregne, and Richard Parker then Bailiffs of the same, Ithel de Byrchoucr, Gilbert the smith, Henry de Pole, and others.

Given at fflynt, 2nd October 20 Edward III. [1346].

No. 54.　　　*Liverpool.*

1355. Fine levied at Lancaster in the Duchy Court on Monday after the Feast of St. Laurence, 5 Henry Duke of Lancaster [17th Aug. 1355], before Thomas de Seton, Henry de Haydok, John Cokeyn, and Roger de Haryngton, Justices, and others, between William de Lyverpull plaintiff and Simon de Walton and Alianor his wife deforciants of a messuage and five acres of land in Lyverpull whereby the premises were acknowledged to belong to the said William, in consideration of which the said William paid to the said Simon and Alianor twenty marks of silver.

No. 55.   *Liverpool.*

1355. Grant from Thomas del Neuport chaplain to William the clerk of Lyverpull and Emme his wife and their joint heirs of a selion of land in Lyverpull which he had of Margery, who was the wife of Hugh de Wisewall, in a certain place called Le Mukel-olde-feld; and failing such heirs, to the heirs of the said William for ever. Witnesses:

William fil. Adam de Lyverpull, John del More, Richard de Aynesargh, Alexander Comyn, Adam fil. Richard, Nicholas Foxe, Robert fil. Mathew, Adam de Longwroa, and others.

Given at Lyverpull on Monday next after the Feast of St. Michael the Archangel [5th Oct.], 29 Edward III. [1355].

Small oval seal of green wax: the Blessed Virgin and Holy Child, surrounded by a legend partly broken away.

No. 56.   *Liverpool.*

1366. John Amorieson of Wygan to Adam fil. Mathew de Kenyan; Bond in ten pounds; the condition being that if Katherine daughter of the said Adam and wife of the said John is alive four years after solemnisation of their marriage, or, she being dead, there is issue male born of the marriage then living, the Bond is to be void.

Done at Lyverpull on Saturday in the week after Easter [11th Apr.], 40 Edward III. [1366]. [In Norman-French.]

No. 57.   *Wigan.*

1365/6. Grant from John fil. Jordan de Shakersley of Wygan to John his son of a toft of land in Wygan situate between the grantor's land and land of John de Longshaw, one end of which abuts on the road leading from Wygan to Hyndley, and the other reaches up to the high [road] of Scoles. Witnesses:

William de Assheton, Mathew Russell, Richard le Lister, Robert le Bacster, William fil. Richard, and others.

Given at Wygan on Sunday next after the Feast of the Conversion of St. Paul [1st Feb.], 40 Edward III. [1365/6].

No. 58.   *Liverpool.*

1366. Grant from Adam fil. Richard de Lyverpull to William fil. Adam de Lyverpull his heirs and assigns of four bovates of land situate a Le Mecul-holde-feld of which two lie together between the lands of Maurice de Galeway and Emme de Sidegreues, and the other two lie together next land of the heirs of Alice de . . . . on the north side. Witnesses :

Richard de Aynesargh, Nicholas the clerk, Robert fil. Mathew, John le Somenor, John fil. Almaric, and others.

Given at Lyverpull on Friday next after the Translation of St. Thomas the Martyr [10th July], 40 Edward III. [1366].

No. 59.   *Liverpool.*

1368/9. Deed poll whereby Richard Jacson Kay of Lyverpull grants to William fil. Adam of Lyverpull a messuage situate in Le Dale stret between the tenements of Robert le Harper and Richard de Aynesargh. Witnesses :

Richard de Aynesargh, John fil. Almaric, William le Child, Nicholas the clerk, John le Somenor, and others.

Given at Lyverpull on Wednesday next before the Feast of St. Hillary [10th Jan.], 42 Edward III. [1368/9].

No. 60.   *Liverpool.*

1368/9. Lease from William fil. Roger del More of Lyverpull to John fil. Almaric of Wygan and his assigns of four bovates of land in the territory of Lyverpull lying next the Castle Orchard, the end of which abuts on the messuage in which Robert de Rouchester formerly dwelt, for a term of ten years from Michaelmas 42 Edward III., at a rent of twelve silver pennies to be paid at Michaelmas yearly. Witnesses :

William fil. Adam de Lyverpull, Richard de Aynesargh, Nicholas the clerk, William le Child, John le Somenor, and others.

Given at Lyverpull on Monday next after the Feast of St. Gregory [13th March], 42 Edward III. [1368/9].

No. 61.   *Liverpool.*

1368. Grant from John fil. Adam the clerk of Lyverpull to William fil. Adam of Lyverpull his heirs and assigns of a plot of ground twenty feet long and seventeen feet wide situate in Le Bonk strete between the tenement of St. Nicholas and land of John de Stanay. Witnesses :

John fil. Almaric, Richard de Aynesargh, William le Child, John le Somenor, Nicholas the clerk, and others.

Given at Lyverpull on Sunday next after the Feast of the Invention of the Holy Cross [7th May], 42 Edward III. [1368].

No. 62. *Liverpool.*

1368. Grant from John Tippup of Lyverpull to Thomas fil. Henry de Stonburlegh his heirs and assigns of a selion of land situate in Le Lytil-holde-feld between land of the heirs of John fil. Adam fil. Simon and land of the heirs of John Baron. Witnesses :

John fil. Almaric, William fil. Adam de Lyverpull, Richard de Aynesargh, William le Child, Nicholas the clerk, and others.

Given at Lyverpull on Thursday next after the Feast of St. James the Apostle [27th July], 42 Edward III. [1368].

No. 63. *Liverpool.*

1369. Grant from Thomas fil. Henry de Stonburley to Roger de Thorneton, chaplain, of a selion of land in Le Litil-holde-feld which the grantor had of John Tippup of Lyverpull. Witnesses :

William fil. Adam de Lyverpull, John Amoryson, Richard de Aynesargh, Nicholas the clerk, William le Child, and others.

Given at Lyverpull on Thursday next before the Feast of St. Margaret the Virgin [19th July], 43 Edward III. [1369].

No. 64. *Liverpool.*

1369. John de fforneby grants by way of Mortgage to John Amoryson of Wygan his heirs and executors half a burgage, as contained by bounds, situate in Le Chapel strete in the town of Lyverpull, for securing repayment of the sum of seventeen pounds. Witnesses :

Richard de Aynesargh, William fil. Adam de Lyverpull, Robert de Lydgate, Stephen le Walshe, Richard Typpupe, and many others.

Given at Lyverpull on Tuesday next before the Feast of St. Mary Magdalene [17th July], 43 Edward III. [1369].

No. 65. *Liverpool.*

1369. Bond whereby John de fforneby binds himself to pay seventeen pounds in silver to John Amoryson or his attorney by equal payments at Lyverpull at the Nativity of Our Lord and the Annunciation of the Blessed Virgin.

Given at Lyverpull on Monday next before the Feast of St. James the Apostle [23rd July], 43 Edward III. [1369].

No. 66.   *Kenyon.*

1369. Agreement between Adam de Kenyan and Katherine, formerly wife of John Almorison, in pure widowhood, witnesseth :

That Katherine agrees that Adam should have the custody of all the goods and chattels of Richard, Nicholas, and Thurstan, sons of the said John and Katherine, namely of the goods and chattels of Richard fifteen pounds of silver, and of Nicholas twenty-five pounds, and of Thurstan fifteen pounds :

And if Richard should die without lawful issue, his goods to remain to his brother Nicholas ;

And if Nicholas should die without such issue his goods to remain to his brother Thurstan ;

And if Thurstan should die without such issue all his goods and chattels to remain over to his brother Richard and his heirs.

Given at Lyverpull on Monday next before the Feast of St. Andrew [26th Nov.], 43 Edward III. [1369].

No. 67.   *Liverpool.*

1370. Grant from Roger fil. William Marioteson of Lyverpull to William fil. Adam of Lyverpull his heirs and assigns of a fourth part of a burgage with buildings thereon situate in Le Dale stret between the tenement of Emme de Sidgreues and the tenement of Emme late wife of Stephen le Corniser.

Also two selions of land of which one lies in Le Ouer-hethi-londes between land of Adam fil. Richard and land of the heirs of William de Sefton And the other lies in the same field in two hallonds between land of the heirs of Eustace the draper and land of Margerie de fforneby. Witnesses :

Richard de Aynesargh, John de Wolleton, John le Somenor, John Tipp[up], Adam le Fourbourg, and others.

Given at Lyverpull on Sunday next after the Feast of St. Luke the Evangelist [20th Oct.], 44 Edward III. [1370].

No. 68.   *Liverpool.*

1306/7. Grant from Robert Clerk of Lyverpull to Richard Mapdurem his heirs or assigns of a landa of ground in the territory of Lyverpull situate in the field called Le Hethylondes between land of the grantor and land of Alan fil. John : And the half burgage situate in Castle street between the tenements of Alice daughter of Adam and Adam fil. Richard will acquit the said landa from the claims of the chief lord of the fee. Witnesses :

John de Mora, Alan Walsemon, William fil. Ralph, William Baron, Roger de Accres, Richard de Mora, and many others.

Given at Lyverpull on Friday in the Octave of the Epiphany [13th Jan.], 35 Edward I. [1306/7].

No. 69. *Liverpool.*

1374. Grant from William le Blake of Lyverpull to William fil. Adam de Lyverpull his heirs and assigns of six selions of land situate in the fields of the town of Lyverpull in different places, of which two lie in Le Hethylondes below the road and one above the road, one other selion lies over against Le Qwyte Crosse, and half a selion is situate in Coupedale, and half a selion lies in Le Quyt-acres, and half a selion at Le Lomelake, and half a selion in Le Morecroftes over against land of the heirs of William Dykeson. Witnesses :

Richard de Aynessargh, John de Hull, John le Somenour, Stephen le Walshe, Nicholas the clerk, and others.

Given at Lyverpull on Tuesday in the Feast of St James the Apostle [1st Aug.], 48 Edward III. [1374].

No. 70. *Liverpool.*

1377. Lease from Hugh de Lyverpull to John de Coupeland and Margaret his wife of a messuage with buildings situate in Le Dale strete between the tenement of the heirs of Richard Tue and the tenement late of Robert fil. Mathew, together with four selions of land situate in different places, of which one is in Le Nether-hethy-londes and abuts on the land of Nicholas the clerk, and another lies in the same field next land of John de Hull, near Le Stote, and two selions lie in Le Mikel-holde-feld, for a term of ten years from the Feast of the Nativity of St. John Baptist, 1 Richard II., at an annual rent of sixteen shillings of silver to be paid on the quarter days usual in the town of Lyverpull ; the premises to be kept in repair against wind and rain by the lessees during the term. Witnesses :

Richard de Aynesargh then Mayor of the town of Lyverpull, Stephen le Walshe, John le Somenor then Bailiffs of the same town ; John de Eccleston, and others.

Given at Lyverpull on Sunday next before the Feast of the Translation of St. Thomas [28th June], 1 Richard II. [1377].

(Small round seal of red wax: a Katherine wheel.)

No. 71.

1378/9. John Parr, Robert Parr, son of the late John, John Wodfall, and Henry Tarlton of the County of Lancaster, gentlemen, to John Parr son and heir of the late Henry Parr, otherwise Henry Halsall.

Arbitration Bond in £20 to abide the Award of James Stanley Archdeacon of Chester the subject of dispute being "specyaly off & for yᵉ Ryght Inᵗest titull & clayme of yᵉ Waᵗ Mylne yᵉ whych yᵉ said John Parr Entendyth to make on his ppur soule grounde wt yᵉ tachement of yᵉ waᵗ to lye on the Comvn in piūdiᵗ hurt & dysheretens of yᵉ aboffe bounden John & Robᵗ & thayre heyres as they clayme so yᵗ yᵉ saydle Ordennce dome Awarde be made & to yᵉ pts delyūd in Writyng by or with yᵉ sayd Sʳ James Stanley archi of Chestᵗ & Arbittʳ enselyt afore yᵉ fest of the Annūciacoñ of our Lady next to come." Dated 11th January, 2 Richard II. [1378/9].

No. 72.   Wigan.

1380. Katherine wife of William fil. Adam de Lyverpull leases to Robert le Jewe of Wygan for his life a certain plot of land which came to her after the death of John fil. Almaric situate in the town of Wygan next the land of the said Robert, in Le Scoles, rendering annually to the grantor and her heirs for the first thirty years of the term eighteen silver pennies by four equal quarterly payments. If the lessee should die before the expiration of the term, his heirs may take on the lease or assign it, and should either he or his assigns wish to hold it after the expiration of the said thirty years, then the annual rent to be twenty shillings in silver paid quarterly, to Katherine and her heirs. Witnesses:

Adam de Byrkeheued, then Mayor, Almaric de Wygan, Henry fil. Almaric, and others.

Given at Wygan on Sunday next after the Feast of St. Katherine the Virgin [2nd Dec.], 4 Richard II. [138c].

Covenant by the lessee that he and his heirs will do repairs during the term.

(Small round seal of green wax: Greek cross in high relief.)

No. 73.   Wigan.

1380/1. Quit-claim from Almaric fil. William le Walker of Wygan to Henry Banastre and William le Jewe, chaplains, of all his right and title in all messuages lands and tenements which they hold of his gift and concession in the town of Wygan. Witnesses :

Adam le Birkhed, then Mayor, Hugh del Crosse, John del Croft, Henry fil. Almaric, and others.

Given at Wygan on Friday next after the Feast of the Purification of Blessed Mary [8th Feb.], 4 Richard II. [1380/1].

No. 74. *Liverpool.*

1382. Deed Poll whereby Sir Adam de Hoghton, Knight, acknowledges to have received from William fil. Adam de Lyverpull and John de ffaryngten the elder, sixteen pounds of silver in part payment of a sum of twenty pounds, in which sum the said William and John were bound to him.

Given at Lyuerpull on the festival of St. Augustine the Confessor [28 August], 6 Richard II. [1382].

No. 75. *Wigan & Leigh.*

1382. Grant from Hugh del Crosse of Wygan to William le Jewe, chaplain, and Thomas le Byrum of all his lands in Wygan and Legh in the County of Lancaster. Witnesses :

Adam de Byrkehed, Mayor of Wygan, Nich de Worthington, Henr. del Marsh, Mathew Russell, William del Wynd, and others.

Given at Wygan on the Friday after the Feast of St. Leonard [13th Nov.], 6 Richard II. [1382].

No. 76. *Wigan.*

1383. Grant by Robert de Blakeburn and William le Jewe, chaplains, to Alice de Clapam for the term of her life, of a plot of land with buildings situate in Le Scoles de Wygan, which they had of the feoffment of Roger de Ines de Wygan, to be held by the said Alice of the lord of the town of Wygan by the services thence due ; and after her death to George son of the said Roger de Ines and heirs male of his body lawfully begotten, remainder to Richard and Ralph, sons of the said Roger and their heirs male in succession, remainder to Nicholas son of Hugh de Ines and his heirs male, remainder to the right heirs of the said Roger. Witnesses :

Adam de Byrkeheued, then Mayor, Hugh del Crosse, Nicholas de Worthyngton, Henr. del Mersh, John de Croft, William del Wynd, Robert de Heghfeld, and many others.

Given at Wygan on Sunday in the octave of St. Luke the Evangelist [25th Oct.], 7 Richard II. [1383].

No. 77. *Liverpool.*

1383. In the Name of God, Amen: I William, son of Adam of Lyverpull, being of sound mind although sick in body, make my Will as follows: In the first place I bequeath my soul to God and blessed Mary the Virgin and all Saints, and my body to be buried in the Chapel of Lyverpull before the figure of the white statue of Mary, where my own proper burial place is provided.

Also, I bequeath three quarters of corn to be distributed in bread on the day of my burying.

Also, I bequeath six pounds of wax about my body.

Also, I bequeath to each priest celebrating in the Chapel of Lyverpull four pence.

Also, I bequeath the residue of all my goods to Katharine my wife and my children born of the said Katharine; and to carry out this Will I appoint as my executors John the fuller, chaplain, and William Parcker, chaplain.

Given at Lyverpull on Tuesday next after the Feast of Saint Luke the Evangelist, in the presence of Thomas del More, then Mayor, and John de Eccleston, and others my neighbours, A.D. one thousand three hundred and eighty-three.

Proved before the Dean of Weryngton, in the Chapel of Lyverpull, on Saturday in the Festival of Saint Barnabas [18th June], 1384.

Inventory of all the goods of William son of Adam of Lyverpull on Tuesday next after the feast of Saint Luke the Evangelist A.D. one thousand three hundred and eighty-three.

In primis: corn in the barn, of the value of ten marks.

Item: Seven dairy cows, of the value of ten shillings each.

Item: two cows, two heifers, and one steer, each of the value of half a mark.

Item: three horses, of the value of one mark each.

Item: eighteen pigs, of the value of thirty shillings.

Item: twenty-five selions of wheat sown, of the value of six pounds.

Item: domestic utensils, of the value of eleven [? eight] marks.

Sum total: forty marks.

No. 78. *Wigan.*

1384
or
1385.

Quit-claim from Margaret, widow of Nicholas de Worthynton, in pure widowhood, to Hugh del Crosse, of certain land in Staneygate in the town of Wygan. Witnesses : Adam de Birkenhed, John del Croft, Thurstan le Bacster, William del Wynde, William de Perbalt. Given at Wygan 8 Richard II. [1384-5]. [Almost illegible.]

No. 79. *Wigan.*

1385.

Acknowledgment by Robert de Derby of having received of Thomas Dicōson de Wygan and Henry del Mershe the sum of twelve pounds four shillings of silver in part payment of a sum of forty-eight pounds sixteen shillings. Given at Weryngton on Friday within the Vigil of the Translation of St. Thomas the Martyr [7th July], 9 Richard II. [1385].

No. 80. *Wigan.*

1386.

Grant from William le Jewe, chaplain, to Almaric le Walker, of Wygan, and Alice, daughter of Adam le Loriner, of Wygan, of all messuages, lands and tenements, with buildings and appurtenances, which he had of the feoffment of the said Almaric, in the town and territory of Wygan, to be held of the chief lord of the fee by the accustomed services : Should the said Alice die without heirs of herself and the said Almaric, the property to go to Almaric and his heirs in perpetuity. Witnesses :
Hugh del Crosse, then Mayor [of Wygan], Adam de Byrkeheued, Mathew Russell, John ffoxe, chaplain, Thomas Cosyn, chaplain, Thurstan le Baxter, and others.
Given at Wygan on Wednesday next after the Annunciation of Blessed Mary the Virgin [28th March], 9 Richard II. [1386].

No. 81. *Liverpool.*

1386.

Power of Attorney from Hugh de Lyverpull, mason, to John de Lynacre, to deliver to John del Morehouse, of Lyverpull, seisin of a quarter of a burgage in Lyverpull.
Given at Lyverpull on Wednesday next before the Feast of St. Margaret the Virgin [18th July], 10 Richard II. [1386].
(Small round seal of green wax : a Latin cross between two palm branches.)

No. 82.   *Wigan.*

1388. Indenture whereby Almaric le Walker leases to Richard
de Longeschagh an acre of land called Le Prestysacre,
lying in Botlingsfeld, in the town of Wygan, between
land of the said Richard and land of Thomas de
Worthyngton : Rendering annually for the first sixteen
years from the date hereof, one Red Rose at the Feast
of the Nativity of St. John Baptist : And if the said
Richard or his assigns should wish to hold the premises
after the expiration of the said sixteen years, then he or
they shall pay to the said Almeric or his heirs a rent of
one hundred shillings in silver yearly : And if the rent,
or any part of it, be in arrear for forty days, the said
Almaric or his heirs shall be at liberty to take and keep
possession for ever : And if the said Richard dies
before the completion of the term, his assigns may take
on the lease for the remainder of the term. Witnesses :
Adam de Byrkeheued, then Mayor [of Wygan],
Thomas de Dokesbury, William le Lyster, and others.

Given at Wygan on Sunday next before the Nativity
of the Blessed Virgin Mary [6th Sept.], 12 Richard II.
[1388].

No. 83.   *Liverpool.*

1390. Grant from John de Hull of Lyverpull to William de
Penereth and Cecilia the grantor's daughter, in free
marriage, their heirs and assigns, of [1] a quarter of a
burgage of land with its buildings in Le Chapell strete,
between the tenements of Thomas Le Coudray and St.
Nicholas of Lyverpull, [2] a quarter of a burgage of
land in Le More strete next the tenement of Robert
del Morehouse, [3] one selion in Le Quytaceres
between the tenements of Thomas del More and
Margerie de Longe, [4] one halland of land in Coupedale between that of said Thomas and John Ball, [5] also
three butts of land next the tenement of John de Lyverpull, [6] two butts of land at the end of the Corkerres-
croft, [7] one selion in the Hethy-landes next to Thomas
del More, [8] one selion there next the tenement of
Sir Robert Kelyng, [9] one selion of land there between
the lands of Thomas le Coudrey and John Bell, [10]
one selion next Euerstan Myln, [10] one selion of land
in Le Mekel-hold-feld abutting against the land of
Nicholas de Lyverpull clerk, [12] one selion of land in
the same field next land of Robert de Seacome towards
the Mill, [13] one landa of ground in Le Shyrreueacres

by the pepper corn: To be held, with Turbary, of the chief lords of the fee by the services due and accustomed for ever. Witnesses:

Thomas de la More, then Mayor of the town of Lyverpull, Richard de Hulm, Thomas le Coudray, Symon de Kyrkedale, William de Roby, and others.

Given at Lyverpull on Friday next after the Feast of the Invention of the Holy Cross [6th May], 13 Richard II. [1390].

(Very small round seal of red wax : a fleur-de-lis.)

No. 84. *Preston.*

1393/4. Power of Attorney from John Gogh, Ithel clerk of Neston, John Doudson, Thomas Dany, John Bumble, Hugh fil. Henry Jonneson and John dil Bonk to Henry dil Mersche of Wygan, to receive seisin of all the lands and tenements which they had of the feoffment of John Amoryson in the county of Lancaster.

Given at Preston on Thursday next after the Feast of the Purification of the Blessed Virgin Mary [4th Feb.], 17 Richard II. [1393/4].

No. 85. *Wigan.*

1396. Indenture shewing that whereas Roger le Coke of Wigan and Alice his wife may have granted to Thomas de Docusbury for ever all lands and tenements in Le Wodhous of Wygan, and although by a Statute Merchant they are bound to pay £20 sterling to said Thomas : Nevertheless, Thomas concedes that if Roger and Alice will pay £3 : 10 : 0 within the next three years, it shall be lawful to the said Roger and Alice to have the said lands and tenements as they had formerly, for ever, the Statute notwithstanding : But, if in default, entry on the land is made, Thomas shall have the crops until St. Martin's in winter, also the expenses of repairs, &c., on the view of four chosen persons : But if Roger and Alice perform the above Covenants the Statute shall be void : Further, that if the lands are in the hands of Thomas for non-payment, William, son of Roger and Alice, shall have power to redeem the same within the said three years. Witnesses :

Adam de Byrkehed, then Mayor [of Wigan], William del Wynde, Roger del More, and others.

Given at Wygan on Sunday next after the Feast of St. Michael the Archangel [1st Oct.], 20 Richard II. [1396].

(Small seal of brown wax: an equilateral triangle, apex downwards, surrounded by a border of pellets.)

No. 86. *Ince, by Wigan.*

1397/8. Grant from Robert fil. William de Ines to William le Jew, chaplain, and Thomas Cosyn, chaplain, of all his messuages, lands, &c. in Ince next Wigan. Witnesses:
Roger de Hulton, John fil. Robert de Laweton, John de Oculshagh, Thomas de Halghton, Henry de Ines, and others.
Given at Ines on Friday after the Epiphany [11th Jan.], 21 Richard II. [1397/8].

No. 87. *Culchith and Kenyon.*

1399. Quit-claim from John de Kynknall to Peter de Kynknall, his brother, of all his right and title to the lands and houses, which Peter has of his gift in Culchith and Kenyan by deed. Witnesses:
Sir William de Atherton, Thomas de Holcroft, Robert de Sotheworth, and others.
Given at Culchyth on Friday before the Feast of All Saints' [31st Oct.], 1 Henry IV. [1399].

No. 88. *Ormskirk.*

1396/7. Power of Attorney from Thomas de Kent, of York, mercer, to Thomas de Dukesbury, of Wygan, to receive of John Myrescogh, of Ormeskirk, thirty-six shillings sterling, as by tally made between them, with power of arrest if necessary.
Given at York 14 February, 20 Richard II. [1396/7].

No. 89. *Culchith and Kenyon.*

1401. Grant from John de Kynkenale to John de Lamley, chaplain, of all his lands and tenements in Culchith and Kenyon, with common pasture and turbary, and reversions, if any. Witnesses:
Henry dil Grene, Thomas Jacson of Culchith, Robert de Sotheworth, Richard de Sutton of Newton, and others.
Given at Culchith on Thursday after the Feast of St. Wilfred [13th Oct.], 3 Henry IV. [1401].
Round seal of red wax: a figure standing between two palm branches, a Katherine wheel in the background.

No. 90. *Culchith and Kenyon.*

1401. John de Kynkenale and Emma, late wife of Adam de Kynkenale, attorn Richard le Pierpoint, Adam Robynson of Lowton, William fficheling and Thomas Jacson of Culchith, to deliver seizin of lands and tenements in Culchith and Kenyan to John Lamley, chaplain.

Given on Friday next after the Feast of St. Wilfred [14th Oct.], 3 Henry IV. [1401].   **1368290**

No. 91.   *Chorley.*

1401. John, son of Sir John Lovell, Knight, Lord of Lovell of Holand [sends] greeting. Whereas Sir John de Lovell, my father, and Matilda his wife, granted to Robert the son of Henry de Burgh all the lands, tenements, woods, and wastes he had in Chorley, called Helegh, to be held of the chief lord of the fee : Know ye that I have confirmed the same to the aforesaid Robert for ever. Witnesses :

Thomas ffleming, Richard de Keygley, Knights, Ralph de Standish, Thomas Bradshagh of Hagh, John de Cophull, and others.

Given in the Feast of the Conception of the Blessed Mary [8th—16th Dec.], 3 Henry IV. [1401].

No. 92.   *Liverpool.*

1401/2. Grant from John del Morehouse of Lyverpull, to Thomas Hardyng of Lyverpull of a quarter burgage in Le Dale strete, between land of Richard de Aynesargh and the King's highway, extending lengthwise from the tenement of the heirs of Henry Tippup to the Milne-dame : To be held of the chief lord of the fee. Witnesses :

Robert de Derby, then Mayor of Lyverpull, John de Lunt and John Dey, then Bailiffs, Thomas del More, John Cole, and others.

Given at Lyverpull on Friday after the Purification of the Blessed Mary [3rd Feb.] 3 Henry IV. [1401/2].

No. 93.
Culchith, Lowton, and Kenyon.

1401/2. Peter de Kynkenale quitclaims and warrants to John de Lamley, chaplain, all his right in the messuages, lands, and tenements which John has of the gift of John de Kynkenale, brother of Peter, in Culchith, Lauton and Kenyan. Witnesses :

William Daas, parson of the Church of Wynwhik, James del Holt, Nicholas de Riseley, Thomas de Ashton and others.

Given on the 12th of February 3 Henry IV. [1401/2].

1402. Robert fil. Henry del Burgh quitclaims to Edward de Chernok and Thomas de Chernok his brother all his right in the lands and tenements which he holds by the feoffment of Sir John de Lovell of Holand and Matilda his wife, in Chorley called Heley. Witnesses:

Hugh de Standish, John de Cophull, Richard de Tunley and others.

Given at Chorley on Tuesday after the Translation of St. Thomas the Martyr [4th July], 3 Henry IV [1402].

Oval seal of red wax; letter B below a crown.

1402/3. Grant from Robert Dyconson and William le Jewe, chaplains, to Richard le Marschall of Wygan Wodhouse, and Isabella his wife, daughter of William de Chysnall, and the lawful heirs of them two, of a plot of land in Wygan Wodhouse, which they hold by the grant of William del Wynd of Wygan, Roger Nevin, chaplain, and John de Hopton: Remainder to Richard Scott of Wygan the younger and the heirs of his body: Remainder to Richard le Marschall and his heirs for ever. Witnesses:

Thomas de Dokesbury, then Mayor of Wygan, Henry del Mersch, Ralph de Standish and others.

Given at Wygan Wodhouse on Sunday after the feast of Saint Chad, bishop [5th March], 4 Henry IV [1402/3].

(Two seals of brown wax; one shewing a figure kneeling before the Blessed Virgin and Holy Child, the other a long cross.)

1402/3. Quitclaim from Edward de Chernok to Thurstan de Anderton, Richard del Crosse and Thomas Trygge, of all his right in the lands and tenements which he had of the feoffment of Robert del Burgh in Chorley called Heley. Witnesses:

Richard de Hoghton, knight, John del Bothe, Ralph de Standysh and others.

Given at Lancaster on the 10th of March, 4 Henry IV [1402/3].

(Small red seal; an eagle's claw.)

1404. Grant from Matilda, cousin and heiress of Robert le Herdemon of Lyverpull, to Richard del Crosse, his heirs and assigns, of a quarter burgage, which she and Robert de Sefton, chaplain, her brother, inherited after the death of Robert le Herdemon, in Le Dale Strete in the town of Lyverpull, between the tenement of the said Richard and that of Gibert le Maryneer : To be held of the chief lords of the fee by the accustomed services. Witnesses :

Thomas del More, then Mayor of the Town of Lyverpull, William del More his son, John de Hull, John [Cole], and Richard le Swyn then Bailiffs of Lyverpull and others.

Given at Lyverpull on Tuesday before St. Barnabas the Apostle [10th June], 5 Henry IV [1404].

No. 98.   *Liverpool.*

1404. Nicholas de Lyverpull, clerk, quitclaims to Richard del Crosse all his right in a quarter burgage in Le Dale strete in the town of Lyverpull, which Richard holds of the feoffment of Matilda de Sefton. Witnesses :

Thomas del More, then Mayor of the town of Lyverpull, John Cole and Richard le Swyn, then Bailiffs of the same town, John Baron, Adam le Barker and others.

Given at Lyverpull on Saturday before the Nativity of St. John Baptist [21st June], 5 Henry IV [1404].

No. 99.   *Eccleshall.*

1404, Power of Attorney from Robert Brydde of Eccleshall to John Bendebowe of Lostok, to demand, seek and recover of Henry de Wynstanley six marks sterling. Witnesses :

William Smerley, John Salvin, Richard Peshale and others.

Given at Eccleshale on Wednesday after St. Katherine [26th Nov.], 6 Henry IV [1404].

No 100.   *Kirkdale.*

1405. Thomas son of John Delyot attorns John de Sallay to give seisin of two sclions in Kirkedale to Richard de Crosse, which he holds of his feoffment by deed.

Given the 25th day of May, 6 Henry IV [1405].

No. 101.   *Liverpool.*

1406. Grant from Nicholas de Lyverpull, clerk, and William de Swynley to Richard del Crosse his heirs and assigns, of one quarter burgage of land in Le Dale strete in the town of Lyverpull, situate between the tenement of the said Richard and that of Robert de Longwro, which

E

quarter burgage is held of the feoffment of Gilbert de
Maryner. Witnesses :

Thomas de More, then Mayor of Lyverpull, John
Dey, Richard del Mosse, then Bailiffs, John de Lynacre,
John Brön, and others.

Given at Lyverpull on Saturday in the third week in
Lent [13th March], 7 Henry IV [1405/6].

No. 102,   Liverpool.

1405/6. Grant from Gilbert le Maryner of Magna Crosby to
Nicholas de Lyverpull, clerk, and William de Swynley
their heirs and assigns, of one quarter burgage of land
in the town of Lyverpull, situate in Le Dale strete,
between the tenements of Richard del Crosse and the
heirs of Robert de Longwro. Witnesses :

Thomas de More, then Mayor of Lyverpull, John
Dey and Richard del Moss, then Bailiffs, John de
Lynacre, John de Sallay, clerk, and others.

Given at Lyverpull on Monday in the second week
of Lent [8th March], 7 Henry IV [1405/6].

No. 103.   Liverpool.

1407.   Grant from Adam le Barker of Lyverpull to William de
Lunt, chaplain, his heirs and assigns, of one quarter burgage with the buildings thereon, situate in Le Dale strete,
between the tenements of John Typope and Roger de
Syggreyne ; also five selions in Lyverpull Field, of which
two lie in Le Wate-hurth between the lands of Robert de
Derby and William fil. Adam ; the third lies between the
lands of John Balle and William fil. Adam in Le Nether-
hethe-londes ; the fourth lies in Kirkdale Field, between
lands of Thomas del More and . . . . ; also of two
hallands, one in Le Crac-folde, between lands of Adam
de Ditton and Robert d'Irland, and the other in Le
Micul-holde-felde, between lands of Thomas de More
and Richard de Blaken : Rendering yearly to [the altar
of] St. Katherine in the Chapel of St. Nicholas two
shillings, and to the Blessed Mary of Walton twelve
pence for ever. Witnesses :

Thomas del More, then Mayor of Lyverpull, John
de Driffeld and John de Sallay, then Bailiffs, Robert de
Derby, John de Lynacre, and others.

Given at Lyverpull the 14th of April, 8 Henry IV
[1407].

No. 104.   Liverpool.

1407.   Surrender by Thomas del Hogh and Katherine his wife
(late the wife of William son of Adam de Lyverpull),

to John de Lyverpull Junior of all their right in a half
burgage in Le Chapel strete of Lyverpull, between
the tenements of Alan Vstasmon and the late Dunkyn
del Denbegh ; also their right in a selion of land in the
Shirreff-acres in Lyverpull Field, between lands of
Richard de Aynessargh and Margaret de More.

Given at Lyverpull on Thursday in the Feast of the
Conception of the Blessed Mary [15 Dec.], 9 Henry IV
[1407].

No. 105. *Liverpool.*

1359. Final Concerd made in the Duchy Court at Preston on
Wednesday before the Feast of St. Michael [25th Sept.],
in the 9th year of Henry, Duke of Lancaster [1359],
before William de Fyncheden, John Cokeyn, Henry de
Haydok, and Roger de Faryngton, Justices, whereby
William son of Adam de Lyverpull obtains from Henry
del Fayreclogh and Margaret his wife one acre of land
in Lyverpull, by payment of forty shillings for the Fine
and Recognizance.

No. 106. *Craunton, &c.*

1409. Grant from John de Craunton, clerk (Rector of the
Parish Church), to John de Lamlay, chaplain (Richard
Crosse his heirs and assigns), and John de Walton, of
all his messuages, lands, and tenements in Craunton,
Wolton, Hale, and Halewode, which he had of the
feoffment of Adam de Craunton. Witnesses :

William (John) de Lagbok, William Bretargh, John
le Drawer, John de Sefton, and others.

Given at Craunton on Monday after the Feast of St.
Chad, Bishop [4th March], 10 Henry IV [1409].

NOTE.—The words in parentheses ( ) are interlineated in the
original, apparently as a rough draft for another charter.

No. 107. *Liverpool.*

1409. Quit-claim from Hugh, clerk, citizen of London, to
Nicholas de Lyverpull, clerk, his heirs and assigns, of
one half burgage in Lyverpull, not built upon, in Le
Dale strete, between the tenements of Richard del
Crosse and William Swyn.

Given at Lyverpull on Monday before the Feast of the
Invention of the Holy Cross [29th April], 10 Henry IV
[1409].

No. 108. *Liverpool.*

1409. Grant from William de Penereth to Nicholas, clerk of
Lyverpull, of his messuages, lands, and tenements in

the town and fields of Lyverpull. Witnesses:

Richard de Moss, Robert Caudray, Robert Seacome, then Bailiffs of the Town of Lyverpull, Richard del Crosse, . . . Thomas Glest, and others.

Given at Lyverpull on Wednesday before the Nativity of St. John Baptist [19th June], 10 Henry IV [1409].

(Small oval seal of red wax: sharp-beaked, crested head of a bird, erased.)

No. 109. *Liverpool.*

1409. Grant from Peter de Ditton to Richard de Crosse of one quarter burgage in Le Dale strete, Lyverpull, between land formerly William Childe's, and land formerly William Swyne's, for thirty years ensuing from Michaelmas next: Rendering yearly one Red Rose on St. John the Baptist's day for all secular demands.

Given at Lyverpull on the Feast of St. John Baptist [24th June], 10 Henry IV [1409].

Octagonal seal of red wax: gothic letter H below a crown.

No. 110. *Liverpool.*

1409. Indenture whereby Nicholas de Lyverpull, clerk, confirms to Richard del Crosse, of Lyverpull, his heirs and assigns, all that messuage, with buildings and other appurtenances, which he had of the feoffment of Peter de Ditton, lying in Le Dale strete, Lyverpull, which was lately William le Child's: Rendering yearly for the first six years one Rose at the Nativity of St. John Baptist, and afterwards three shillings and four-pence, in silver; also rendering to the Mayor and Comonalty of Lyverpull three shillings, in silver, at Christmas and the Nativity of St. John Baptist, for all services. Witnesses:

Robert de Derby, then Mayor of the town of Lyverpull, Robert Coudray, Robert de Seacome, then Bailiffs of the same town, John de Lynacre, John de Sallay, and others.

Given at Lyverpull, on Monday after the Translation of St. Thomas the Martyr [8th July] 10 Henry IV [1409]. Permission to take distraint if the payments fall in arrear.

No. 111. *Liverpool.*

1409. Counterpart of No. 110.

Small oval seal of green wax: a finely cut fleur-de-lis, surrounded by a legend (undecipherable).

1409. Deed Poll, whereby John de Craunton, Rector of the Parish Church of Werinton [Warrington], acknowledges that he is bound to Richard del Crosse in the sum of twenty marks sterling, to be paid at Christmas next.

Given on Monday, in the Feast of Saint Simon and Saint Jude [4th November] 11 Henry IV [1409].

The condition of the bond was to hold Richard del Crosse indemnified against all claims to four acres of land in Craunton. [Condition in Norman-French.]

1409. A similar bond, of the same parties and date, but payable on the Feast of the Purification.

1410. Grant from Richard del Crosse, of Lyverpoll, to Thurstan de Anderton and Henry de Bretherton, chaplains, their heirs and assigns, of all his lands and tenements in Lyverpull, Wygan, Hale, Halewood, Magna Wolveton, aud Kirkedale; also the reversion of all the lands coming to him after the death of Katherine del Hogh, his mother, in Lyverpull and Wygan. Witnesses:

John de Osbaldeston, Robert de Derby, Nicholas, the clerk, Thomas Caudrey, Robert Coudray, and others.

Given at Liverpool, on Monday after the Feast of St. Barnabas the Apostle [16th June], 11 Henry IV [1410].

1410. Grant from John de Sallay to Henry de Mossok, his heirs and assigns, of three selions of his land in Lyverpool Field, viz., two in Coupedale, next the sea, between lands of the heirs of Richard Baron on the south, and of the heirs of Robert de Secom on the north; and one selion in Le Chires-acres between land of Nicholas the clerk and land of Robert de Derby. Witnesses:

John Osbalston, Robert de Derby, John Lynacre, Thomas Caudera, Thomas . . . . , and others.

Given at Lyverpull, on Friday after the Feast of St. John Baptist [27th June], 11 Henry IV [1410].

1410. The King's Writ to the Chancellor of the County Palatine of Lancaster, commanding him to summon, under the seal of the Duchy, and under a penalty of 100 marks,

F

the following persons, viz., Nicholas de Longford, chevalier, John Radclyf, of Ordesale, chevalier, Ralph de Prestwyche, Thurstan de Holand, and Otho Redyth, to appear at Westminster, within the Octave of St. Hillary, to receive the orders of the Court. Witness :

The King himself, at Westminster, 8th November, in the 12th year of his reign [1410]. Wymbysshe.

No. 116. Chorley.

1412. Grant from John de Dokesbury and John del Wroo to Thurstan de Anderton, Richard del Crosse, and Thomas Twygge, of all the messuages, burgages, lands, tenements, woods, and pastures, which they held of the feoffment of the said Thurstan de Anderton and Robert de Anderton, in Chorley, called Heley. Witnesses :

Henry de Chernok, Gilbert de Longtre, Richard de Worthington, and others.

Given at Chorley, on Monday after the Feast of St. Michael [3rd October], 13 Henry IV [1412]. ˙

No. 117. Liverpool.

1410. Grant from Robert de Derby and Elizabeth, his wife, to Richard del Crosse, his heirs and assigns, of the reversion of two half butts of land, lying in the Wallefeld, between lands of Robert de Seacome and lands late of Robert de Longwro, after the decease of Elene, late wife of Richard de Aynesargh, which she held in dower : Rendering yearly four pence in silver at Michaelmas, with power of distraint for non-payment. Witnesses :

John de Osbaldston, then Mayor of Lyverpull, John de Bykerstath and Richard Taillor, Bailiffs of the same town, Thomas Caudray, John de Lynacre, William de Swynley, and others.

Given at Lyverpull, on Monday after the Feast of St. Hillary [20th January], 12 Henry IV [1410].

No. 118. Liverpool.

1411. Grant from Nicolas de Lyverpull, clerk, to Richard del Cross, his heirs and assigns, of all the lands which he held by the feoffment of William de Penereth in Lyverpull Town and Field, except a quarter burgage in Le More strete, next land of the heirs of Robert del Morehouse, which Thomas de Glest holds by the feoffment of the said Nicholas ; except also one land of ground in the Hethy-londes, between lands of Thomas le Coudray and John Bell, which land Nicholas gave to the Chantry of the Blessed Mary of Lyverpull, to celebrate for the soul of William de Penereth. Witnesses:

Robert de Derby, then Mayor of Lyverpull, Thomas de Caudray, John de Lynacre, John le Dey, and Robert de Holand, then Bailiffs of the same town, and others.

Given at Lyverpull, on Sunday in the Feast of All Saints [1st November], 13 Henry IV [1411].

No. 119. Parr.

1412. Quitclaim from Margaret, daughter of Richard de Parr, of Shagh, to Alice, who was the wife of Richard de Parr, of Shagh, for her life, of all right in those messuages and tenements which the said Alice had in Parr; Saving always to the grantor (Margaret) and her heirs her interest in the same after the death of the said Alice. Witnesses:

John de Eltonhead, Henry de Atherton, Henry le Norreys, and others.

Given at Parr, on Wednesday in the Feast of the Conversion of St. Paul [26th January], 14 Henry IV [1412].

No. 120. Liverpool.

1412. Katherine del Hogh, formerly the wife of William, son of Adam de Lyverpull, in her pure widowhood, grants and surrenders to her son John de Lyverpull, Junior. all her estate in one Wind Mill and three selions of land adjoining in Lyverpull, also one plot of land, called Le Taverne, in Le Bonke strete, between the tenement of Richard de Stanay and the tenement of St. Nicholas. Witnesses:

Robert de Derby, then Mayor of Lyverpull, John de Osbaldston, Nicholas the clerk, John del Hogh, and others.

Given at Lyverpull on Monday after the Feast of the Annunciation of Blessed Mary the Virgin [28th March], 13 Henry IV [1412].

Octagonal seal of red wax: on a heater-shaped shield, and extending above it, a merchant's mark.

No. 121. Liverpool.

1412. Grant from John de Lyverpull, Junior, to Robert del Crosse, his heirs and assigns, of a Wind Mill and three selions of land in Lyverpull, also of a plot of land, called Le Tanñe, in Le Bonke street, between the tenement of Richard del Stanay and St. Nicholas. Witnesses :

Robert de Derby, then Mayor of Lyverpull, John de Osboldston, Nycholas the clerk, John del Hogh, and others.

Given at Lyverpull, on Thursday after the Feast of the Annunciation of Blessed Mary the Virgin [31st March], 13 Henry IV [1412].

Oval seal of red wax : Blessed Virgin and Holy Child, encircled by a legend (illegible).

No. 122.   *Liverpool.*

1412.   Grant from John Forneby, brewer, of London, nephew and heir of William Swyn, of Forneby, to Richard del Crosse, his heirs and assigns, of all his messuages and tenements in Lyverpull, which by hereditary right came to him on William Swyn's death.   Witnesses :

John Tippup, mercer, of London ; William Lyverpull, girdeler, of London ; Richard Kynarton, girdeler, of London ; and others.

Given at London, on Friday after the Purification of Blessed Mary the Virgin [4th February], 14 Henry IV [1412].

Small round seal of green wax ; the winged lion of St. Mark.

No. 123.   *Liverpool.*

1412.   Quitclaim from Nicholas de Lyverpull, clerk, to John le Dey, of Lyverpull, his heirs and assigns, of one land of ground, lying between the Crosses, next the Shootsacres, which Gilbert de Everton holds by the devise of Matilda de Sefton and the above Nicholas. Witnesses :

Robert de Derby, then Mayor of Lyverpull, Thomas de Bold, and Roger de Holand, then Bailiffs of Lyverpull, Hugh de Botyll, Thomas de Gleest, and others.

Given at Lyverpull, in the third week of Lent [4-10 March], 14 Henry IV [1412].

No. 124.

1415.   Acknowledgment by John fil. Robert de Workesley of the receipt of six pounds, from Lawrence le Wareyn, by the hands of Richard del Crosse, in part payment of a larger sum, in which Lawrence and others are bound by a bond in writing.

Given on Thursday in the Feast of St. Peter ad Vincula [8th August], 3 Henry V [1415].

No. 125. *Liverpool.*

1416. Grant from Katharine del Hogh, formerly wife of William fil. Adam de Lyverpull, to Richard del Crosse, her son, his heirs and assigns, of all her estate in those messuages, lands, tenements, windmill, fishery, turbary, and common pasture, which William and Katharine held of the feoffment of John de Henthorn and Richard Munn, in the towns of Liverpool and Kirkdale. Witnesses:

Henry de Mosok, William de Swynley, Hugh de Botehull, Thomas Glest, and others.

Given at Lyverpull, on Thursday before the Feast of St. Laurence [7th August], 4 Henry V [1416].

Impression from an antique seal in green wax : a suit of armour.

No. 126. *Wigan.*

1416/7. Quitclaim from Katherine, late wife of Hugh del Cros, of Wygan, to Thomas de Birome and William Jewe, chaplain, their heirs and assigns, of all the messuages, lands, and tenements, which the said Thomas and William hold by the feoffment of Hugh, her late husband, in Leght [? Leigh]. Witnesses:

Hugh del Marsh, then Mayor of Wigan, Adam de Birkhened, of the same town, Henry de Birkhened, son of the said Adam, John de Birkhened, son of the said Henry, Amore Walker, Henry de Birome, and many others.

Given on Saturday after the Feast of the Circumcision, [2nd January, 1417], 4 Henry V [1416/7].

No. 127. *West Derbyshire.*

1420/1. Richard Botiller, of Kirkland, Escheator of the Lord the King, commands the Bailiff of [West] Derbyshire, within 40 days, to summon 24 free and lawful men, of [West] Derbyshire, by a Writ of *Diem clausit extremum* concerning Henry de Scaresbrek and Nicholas de Atherton, deceased ; And to warn Richard del Crosse, that he appear before the Escheator at the same time and place, to shew cause why the lands and tenements of Thomas Dokesbury, an outlaw, ought not to be in the King's hands.

Given on the 16th day of February, 8 Henry V [1420/1].

No. 128. *Liverpool.*

1424. Grant from John de Wolton to Henry de Bretherton, Gilbert Gelibrond, and Thomas Bonnell, of Lyverpull, chaplains, of all his messuages, lands, tenements, rents, reversions, and services, and all his goods and chattels ; Also of the messuage, lands, and tenements which John de Lynacre holds for life, and which after his decease will revert to the grantor and his heirs, and shall then come to the said Henry, Thomas, and Gilbert, chaplains, their heirs and assigns. Witnesses : Robert del More, then Mayor of Lyverpull, Richard Crosse, Henry Mosok, William Swynley, Hugh de Bothull, and others.

Given at Lyverpull, 14th of May, 2 Henry VI [1424]. Oval seal of red wax : an iris.

No. 129.   *Burscough.*

1425. Bond, given by Roger Carter of Burscogh, and Nicholas de Aikscogh of Lathum, to David Gelibront and Charles Gelibront, in ten marks sterling, to be paid on the Feast of the Invention of the Holy Cross next ensuing.

Dated 16th April, 3 Henry VI [1425].

Endorsed : The condition of this bond is that if Richard Carver [Carter] shall well and faithfully serve Charles Gelibront for half a year from 15th May, and yield to the said Charles a third part of his perquisites in foreign parts, he will indemnify Richard during his absence in regard to the king and his officers.

No. 130.   *Liverpool.*

1426. Grant from John de Stanley, chevalier, Henry de Byrum, and Robert de Anderton, to Roger de Chernok and John de Assheton, of Budston, their heirs and assigns, of all the messuages, burgages, lands, tenements, mill, rent, and services which they hold in the towns of Lyverpull, Kirkdale, Wolton, Halewood, Wigan, Holland, Coppull, Heth-Chernok, Heley, and elsewhere in the county of Lancaster, by the feoffment of Thurstan de Anderton, and John de Dokesbere. Witnesses : Henry Blundell [of Ince], Thomas de Bradshagh, of Hagh, William de Worthyngton, Thurstan de Holcroft, Mayor of Lyverpull, John de Byrkeheyde, Mayor of Wigan, and others.

Given at Lyverpull, on Thursday in the fourth week of Lent [14th March, 1426], 4 Henry VI [1426].

No. 131.

1427. Bond in £20 from William fil. Roger le Coke [the cook] to Richard del Crosse, to be paid at Christmas.

Dated Monday after the Feast of the Assumption
of the Blessed Mary the Virgin, [18th August],
5 Henry VI [1427]. Award :
Condition : To abide the order of Laurence Standish
in all matters, real or personal, in dispute between them.
Small seal of green wax : crowned Lombardic letter
M, between branches of a tree.

No. 132.   *Kenyon.*

1418/19.   This endentur' beres wyttenes yat Riĉ of the Crosse,
on of the executores of Maykin, of Kenyan, has delyûe,
to Wiłłm, the son of Maykyn, the hernes yat was of the
forsaid Maykynnes, the whech was in kepyng of the
forsaid Riĉ, in p'cence of Sir John of Stanley, knyght,
James of Strangwais, and other, at Loncastr' the Thursday next before the fest of the Anûnciacõn of oure
Lady [23rd March, 1419], in the yere of kyng Henr',
the son of kyng Henr' [IV.] the seuent, yat is to wete :—
A muche Maser haîtet, baslard hernesshet wyth siluer,
a girdell of siluer, barret wyth lokkes and racches of
siluer, and a nothir girdell of siluer, barret thurgh-oute,
a coler all of siluer, six bosses for a Jak of siluer, with
faure poyntes of silke and siluer, a tabull enewmolte of
siluer, w' a purse of veluet, and a payre of bedes of
whyt aumbr'.
In the wyttenes of the whech thyng the forsaid Sir
John, James of Strangwais, and Wiłłm of Kenyan,
hauen set to hor sealles.
Wretyn at Lancastr' the day and the yere before said.
One seal left : an eagle rising with wings extended.

No. 133.   *Liverpool.*

1429.   Quitclaim from Robert Caudray, of Lyverpull, to Richard
del Crosse, of all his right in one selion of land in le
Dale-feld, in the said town, which selion Richard holds
by the grantor's feoffment.
Given at Lyverpull, on Monday after the Feast of
St. Laurence [15th August], 7 Henry VI [1429].
Small seal of red wax : a merchant's mark.

No. 134.   *Liverpool: Chorley.*

1432.   Johanna de Kenyan, late wife of John de Lyverpull,
quitclaims to Richard del Crosse, his heirs and assigns,
all her rights in all her lands, tenements, woods, water
mill, &c., within Heley, in the town of Chorley, viz. :

the south part of Heley, now in Richard's possession:
Witnesses :

Henry de Mosok, Robert Caudray, Hugh de Botell,
Richard Tippup, and others.

Given at Lyverpull, on Monday after the octave of
the Pasch [5th March], 10 Henry VI [1432].

Small seal of green wax : five pellets arranged in
form of a cross.

No. 135.

1434. Hugh de Botehull to Richard del Crosse, and Thomas
son and heir of the said Hugh.

Bond in £20 to make a sufficient estate to his said
son Thomas of lands purchased of John de Walton.

Dated at . . . . .

Small seal of red wax : crowned Lombardic letter H,
between branches of a tree.

No. 136.

So faded as to be illegible.

No. 137.   *Liverpool.*

1436. John de Stanley, knight, quitclaims to Richard del Crosse
of Lyverpull, all actions or claims of debt from the
beginning of the world to this day.

Given at Lathum, on Thursday after the Feast of All
Saints [8th November], 14 Henry VI [1436].

No. 138.   *Wigan.*

1436/7. Quitclaim from William, son of Roger Coke of Wygan
to Richard del Crosse, and Margaret, his wife, their
heirs and assigns, of all actions, real and personal,
from the beginning of the world to this day.

Dated Monday after the Feast of St. Hillary [14th
January, 1437], 15 Henry VI [1436/7].

No. 139.   *Liverpool.*

1439. Indenture witnessing that Elianore, late wife to Hugh of
Botyll, and Richard of ye Crosse, guardian to Hugh
Thomasson of Botyll, have delivered to Roger of Chernok, as for a mene firende and a trewe, certens dedes,
endentures, &c., viz. :—

1. Deed between John of Lynacre and Robert of
   Bowland and Thomas Bonell, priests.

2. Release by said John to said Robert and Thomas,
   priests.

3. Deed between the same parties.

4. Deed between Robert of Bowland and Thomas Bonell, priests, and Henry of Bretherton, priest, and Richard of yᵉ Crosse.

5. Letter of Attorney: Robert and Thomas, priests, to Robert yᵉ Caudray, to deliver possession.

6. Letter of Attorney, empowering the said Henry, priest, and the said Richard to receive possession.

7. Deed between John of Lynacre and Henry of Bretherton, priest, and Richard of the Crosse.

8. Deed between Henry of Bretherton, priest, and Richard of the Crosse and Hugh de Botill.

9. Deed between William of the Lunt, priest, and John of Lynacre and Jelian, his wife.

10. Fine between the said William the priest, and the said John and Jelian.

11. Release to Hugh of Botyll, by John of Lynacre.

12. Deed between John Johnson Adamson, of Derby, and John of Lynacre.

13. Deed between Hugh of Botyll and Henry of Bretherton, and Thomas Bonell, priests.

Written at Lyverpull, 5th March, 17 Henry VI [1439]. [In English.]

No. 140. *Chorley.*

1441. Indenture whereby a variance between Richard of ye Crosse, on the one part, and John Gelebront and Elizabeth, his mother, on the other part, is settled by the arbitration of Richard of Longtree and Oliver of Anderton, as follows:—John and Elizabeth are to make a Fine in the King's Court to Richard of ye Crosse, of lands in the North parts of the Eves-hey and Eves-field in the town of Chorley; Also John and Elizabeth shall swear on a book that there is no incumbrance on the lands when seisin is given to Richard of ye Crosse; Also that Richard shall resign all claim to the south part of Eves-feld and Eves-hey, and to swear on a book to pay to John 46ˢ 8ᵈ, viz., 26ˢ 8ᵈ at the Feast of St. Luke, and 20ˢ at the Feast of the Ascension of our Lord.

Given the 10th day of October, 20 Henry VI [1441]. Fragments of two small seals. [In old English.]

No. 141. *Liverpool.*

1442. Letter of Attorney from William Nayler and Thomas Bonell, chaplain, empowering Richard del Ford to accept seisin of a messuage, lands, tenements, and windmill, which they have by the feoffment of Richard del Crosse, in the towns of Wigan and Liverpool.

Given on the Feast of St. Barnabas [June 11],
20 Henry VI [1442].

Seal of red wax : small Lombardic letter II.

No. 142.   Liverpool.

1459. Quitclaim from John More, of Lyverpull, and Richard
Dwerehows, of Hale-wood, to John Crosse, of all their
right in two selions of land, which he holds by their
concession. Witnesses :

John Wolton, Jacob Harebron, Hugh Harebron,
and others.

Given at Lyverpull, on the 15th day of August,
37 Henry VI [1459].

Small seal of red wax : a pelican in her piety.

No. 143.   Kenyon.

1416. Roger Banastre acknowledges the Receipt of ten marks
from Mathew de Kenyon, Receiver of the King in the
Duchy of Lancaster, granted him for life, payable at
Easter and Michaelmas.

Dated 4th March, 4 Henry V [1416].

No. 144.   Lathum.

1464/5. Indenture between Alianora Stanley and Jamys S[tanley],
clerk, on the one part, and Rowland fil. Eustas, knight,
and Elizabeth his wife, on the other part, whereby Alianora and James promise to maintain and aid John Crosse
in all the lands and tenements that Rowland hath in
right of his wife, so that if any attempt be made to
molest any of Rowland's tenants, Alianora and James
will see they have lawful redress, and for this Rowland
agrees to give yearly during his espousals with Elizabeth
a Robe of Ireland, or 40s., to be paid by the hands of
John Crosse.

Given at Lathum, the 18th of January, 4 Edward IV
[1464/5].   [In old English].

Two small seals of red wax, each bearing a hart
lodged.

No. 145.   St. Asaph.

1468. James Stanley, clerk, custodian of all the spiritualities
and temporalities of the diocese of St. Asaph (Assanen),
lets to farm, to Howell ap Jenn Vaughan, the Church
of Llannassaph, Assanen, in the said diocese, from the
Feast of the Apostles Philip and James, for one year :
Rendering to the above James £16 at the Feast of the

Apostles Peter and Paul; Howell to bear all the burdens for that time.
Dated the 18th of May, 1468.

No. 146.   *Pemberton.*

1470. Hugh Worsley grants a full receipt for all arrears on account of a messuage, lands, and tenements, in Pemberton, to John, the son of Hugh Pemberton.
Dated the 8th of October, 10 Edward IV [1470]. [Imperfect.]

No. 147.   *Liverpool.*

1470. Bond in £40 given by Richard Gillibrond, of Lathum, Nicholas Hyton, and Gilbert Burscogh, of the county of Lancaster, to John Crosse, of Lyverpull, to be paid at the Feast of the Nativity of St. John the Baptist: The condition is that Richard shall observe the Covenants in a Deed of Marriage between Edmond Gilibrond, his son and heir, and Margaret Crosse.
Given on the 18th of December, 10 Edward IV [1470].
Seal of red wax: two swords saltire-wise, points downwards.

No. 148.   *Liverpool.*

1471. Bond in £100, given by Dame Elenor Longton, of Wygan, Henry Longton, her son and heir, and Richard Birkenhead, son and heir of Henry Birkenhead, of Wygan, to John Crosse, of Lyverpole, to be paid at the Nativity of the Blessed Mary the Virgin.
Given on the 6th of July, 11 Edward IV [1471].
The condition of the bond being that Dame Elenor and Henry shall abide by the award of Edmund Crosse and Henry Birkenhead, Arbitrators, as to all differences concerning lands in Wigan, to this date between Dame Elenor and Henry, on the one part, and John Crosse of Lyverpole, on the other part: The award to be given under seals before the Feast of the Assumption

No. 148*.   *Liverpool.*

1471. Award made by Edmund Crosse and Henry Birkenhead, Arbitrators between John Crosse, of Lyverpole, on the one hand, and Dame Elenor Longton, and Henry Longton, her son and heir, on the other part, awarding to each party certain lands in Wigan.
Given on Monday, before the Feast of the Assumption of Our Lady the Virgin [12th August], 11th Edward IV [1471].

1472.   Grant from John Wodes, and Alice his wife, of Lyverpull,
to John Crosse, of one selion of land, called Le Dobul
lond, lying between the Crosses, in the field of Lyverpull, viz. two hallands lying upon the road leading to
the Breke, and one halland on the same road, between
the selion, late of Derby, on the north, and land of the
late John More, on the south. Witnesses :
Hugh Harebron, then Mayor of Lyverpull, Robert
More, Roger Walton, and others.
Given at Lyverpull, on the 20th day of May,
12 Edward IV [1472].

1472.   Quitclaim from John Wodes, of Lyverpull, and Alicia,
his wife, to John Crosse, of Lyverpull, of all their right
in one selion of land in the field of Lyverpull, as per
charter given to the said John Crosse, and of which he
is in full possession.
Given at Lyverpull, the 21st of May, 12 Edward IV
[1472].

c. 1472.   Quitclaim from John Wodes, of Lyverpull, to John
Crosse, of all his right and title to two selions of land
in the Galow-ffeld, in the field of Lyverpull. Witnesses:
Robert More, Roger Walton, and Robert Swyndeley.

1472/3.   Bond in £20 from Nicholas ffazakerley, son and heir
of William ffazakerley, of the county of Lancaster,
gentleman, to John Crosse, of Lyverpull, to be paid at
Michaelmas.
Given on the 20th day of February, 12 Edward IV
[1472/3].
The Condition of the bond is that Nicholas shall
make a sufficient feoffment and release unto John
Crosse of a burgage in Le Dale Strete, lying between
the tenement of the said John and that of Robert of
Preston, after the decease of William ffazakerley, his
father.
Small oval seal of red wax : a pentacle within a
circle. [In English.]

1473.   Quitclaim from John Wodes, of Lyverpull, to John
Crosse, of Lyverpull, of all his right in one tenement

in Lyverpull, as in a charter conveying it to John Crosse
more fully appears. Witnesses .

Robert More, Christopher Dey, Richard Secum, and
many others.

Given at Lyverpull, on the 1st of June, 13 Edward IV [1473].

Curious seal of brown wax : Lombardic lettter T
and a holly leaf.

No. 154.　　　　　　Liverpool.

1473. Grant from Nicholas ffazakerley, son and heir of William
ffazakerley, late of Kyrkeby, co. Lanc. to John Crosse,
of Lyverpull, of one plot of land, burgage in Le
Dale strete, in the town of Lyverpull, lying between
the burgage of the said John on the west and that of
Robert Preston on the east. Witnesses :

John Davenport, then Mayor of the said Town,
Robert Swyndeley and Thomas Wodeley, then Bailiffs,
Hugh Harebron, Thomas Harebron, and many others.

Given at Lyverpull on the 20th of December, 13
Edward IV [1473].

No. 155.　　　　　　Liverpool.

1473. Quitclaim from Nicholas ffazakyrley, son and heir of
William ffazakerley, late of Kyrkeby, co. Lanc., of all
his right in a plot of land, or burgage, in Lyverpull,
now in his full possession, as by a charter more fully
appears.

Given at Lyverpull, the 24th day of December,
13 Edward IV [1473].

Small seal of brown wax : a fleur-de-lis.

No. 156.　　　　　　Liverpool.

1489 Grant from Henry Botyll, of Kirkdale, to John Crosse, of
Lyverpull, of one selion of land in the field of
Lyverpull, in Le Wayte-yorth [White Earth], between
the selion of Robert More, on the south, and that of
Robert Mosse, on the north : And Henry appoints
John Wisewall to be his attorney in giving seisin to
John Crosse. Witnesses :

Thomas Eves, Thomas Harebrowne, and Richard
Wisewall, with many others.

Given at Lyverpull, on the 20th of June, 4 Henry VII
[1489].

No. 157.　　　　　　Walton.

1494. Bond in £40 given by James Molyneux, Rector of the
Church of Sefton, Laurence Molyneux, his brother, and

Agnes, his sister, the wife of Edmund Winstanley, to Richard Crosse of Walton, to be paid at Pentecost.

Dated on the 9th of June, 9 Henry VII [1494].

The Condition of the bond being that James Molyneux, parson of the parish church of Sefton, shall truly perform the Covenants in a pair of Indentures of the above date, made between the said James and Richard.

No. 158.   Wavertree.

1497. Grant from William Brown, of Penketh, to John Crosse, of Lyverpole, of a parcel of land in the Lordship of Wartre, in the occupation of John Plombe, also of land occupied by Henry Milner, also of another parcel occupied by John Pasmyth, and of a parcel in James Hiton's occupation ; And the grantor appoints Robert Lake his Attorney to give seisin to John Crosse. Witnesses :

John Toxtath, Nicholas ffasacerley, and John Pasmyth, with others.

Given at Waretre, the 10th of July, 12 Henry VII [1497].

Small seal of red wax, shewing initials T.P. below a crown.

No. 159.   Wavertree.

1497. Grant from William Brown, of Penketh, to John Crosse, of Lyverpull, of a parcel of land in the Lordship of Wartr', in the tenure of Henry Elison : And the grantor appoints Robert Lake to be his Attorney to give seisin to John Crosse. Witnesses :

Nicholas ffasakirly, John Toxtath, James Toxtath, and others.

Given at Wartre on the 7th of July, 12 Henry VII [1497].

No. 160.   Wavertree.

1497. Quitclaim from Gilbert, son and heir apparent of William Brown, to John Crosse, of Lyverpole, of all his right and title in the lands which William his father sold to John Crosse, who is now in full possession thereof. Witnesses :

Nicholas ffazacreley, John Pasmith, and others.

Given at Wartr' on the 14th of July, 12 Henry VII [1497].

No. 161.

Liverpool and West Derby.

1497/8. Grant by Nicholas, son of Elizabeth ffazakerley, late wife of William ffazakerley, of Kirkeby, to John Crosse, of Lyverpull, of his reversion, after his mother's death,

in a plot of land called Snodam in [West] Derby, in the occupation of Roger Burgess. Witnesses :
William More, Thomas Ewys, Richard Wyswall, and others.
Given at Lyverpull on the 7th of March, 13 Henry VII [1497/8].

No. 162.
Charnok, Chorley, and Speke.

1498. Grant from Robert Chernoke, Esq., to Henry Crichelawe, chaplain, William Michael, Thomas Lawrence, Esq., Hugh Adlington, and George Tarleton, of a messuage in Chernok-Richard, late in the tenure of Christopher Ryding ; also of a messuage in Chorley occupied by William Hyndesley ; of another messuage in Chorley, in the tenure of John Carlill ; of one other messuage in Chorley, in the tenure of William Thomson ; of one messuage in Chernok, occupied by Jacob Hayle ; of one close of land, in Asteley and Chorley, called the Judland ; of eight acres of meadow in Rugh-Asteley and Chorley ; also of meadow and pasture lands in Speke, lately held by Jacob Whitlyng, William Chaloner, junior, William Penulton, Robert Glest, William Chaloner, senior, Tho. Stevynson, Tho. Penulton, Will. Nicholson, Jacob Plombe, Tho. Mercer, Henr' Jenkynson ; and of a messuage in Speke, lately held by Will. Witlyng :
Also he confirms to the above an annual rent of 4s. issuing from land and a tenement of Tho. Hyndesley's in Chernok Richard ; an annual rent of 3s. 7d., from land, &c., of Jacob Bank, in the same place ; an annual rent of 3s. from land, &c, of Oliver Chernok, in the same place :
Robert and Margery, his wife, to hold for their lives, then to the right heirs of Robert : If disturbed, the feoffes may sell for the use of Robert and Margery : And the said Robert Chernoke appoints Will. Calson and Edm. Hoghe his attorneys to give seisin. Witnesses :
Roger Syngleton, John Calvert, Richard Burscoghe, gent., and others.
Dated the 26th of March, 13 Henry VII [1498].

No. 163.   *Huyton.*

1500/1. George, son and heir of Edmund Lathum, of Knowsley, (E)van Haghton, of Lyverpull, John Mercer, of Lathum, and Ralph Bury, son and heir of Thomas

Bury, of Roby, to Richard Crosse, of Walton, son and
heir of John Crosse, of Lyverpull, Esq.   .   .

Bond in £40. Dated 20th February, 16 Henry VII
[1500/1].

Condition : To keep Richard Crosse harmless "anen-
dez" Hamnet Haryngton, by reason of an Obligation
in which Richard is bound with John Bellerby, of
Huyton, to the said Hamnet in £40, touching a rent
for lands in Huyton.

Two seals of brown wax : on one of them a rude
letter M.

No. 164.   Liverpool.

1502.   Grant from Richard Crosse, son and heir of John
Crosse, of Lyverpull, to William Crosse, his brother,
and son of the said John, of one tenement, with houses
and gardens, in le Dale strete, in Lyverpull, in the
tenure of Henry Piombe, and of two buildings with
chambers, next the Cross in the said Town. Witnesses :

James Molyneux, rector of Sefton, John Ireland, kt.,
William More, esq., Thomas Eyvys, David Griffith,
William Bolton, chaplain, William Harebrowne, and
others.

Given at Lyverpull on the 10th September, 18 Henry
VII [1502].

No. 165.   Holand.

1504.   Grant from Agnes Crosse, late wife of John Crosse, in
pure widowhood, to Hugh, son of Hngh Tunstall, of a
messuage, with lands, tenements, meadows, and pastures in Holand, for the life of said Agnes ; Rendering
yearly to the grantor eight shillings at Christmas and
the Nativity of St. John Baptist : Power of distress
if rent be 24 days in arrear. Witnesses :

John Birkenhed, Richard Faireclogh, Richard Taberner, and others.

Given the 7th of November, 20 Henry VII. [In
English].

No. 166.   Heley.

1504/5.   Thurstan Anderton, Esq., and Oliver Anderton, his son
and heir apparent, to Richard Crosse, Esq. Bond in
two hundred pounds, payable at the Nativity of St.
John Baptist.

Dated 3rd of March, 20 Henry VII [1504/5].

Condition : To abide the award of " Maister John
" Chaloner, mon of lawe," concerning the right and
title to certain lands and tenements called Heley,

within the Lordship of Chorley; the award to be delivered before Easter.

Seal of red wax : on a heater-shaped shield an old English letter c.

No. 167. Liverpool.

1505. Quitclaim from . . . ., late wife of John Crosse, of Lyverpull, to Master John Crosse, clerk, executor of the Will of the said John Crosse, Esq., deceased, Richard Crosse, gent., and William Crosse, brother of the said John Crosse, in respect of all actions or quarrels of Richard Crosse, gent., and William Crosse, his brother, John Crosse, clerk, and Richard Crosse, gent., on account of any title or claim she had at her late husband's death.

Dated 13th of August, 20 Henry VII.

No. 168. Liverpool.

1505. John Ireland, late of Hale, in the county of Lancaster, knt., to Richard Crosse, late of Lyverpull, Esq. Bond in four pounds, payable at Easter. Dated 24th December, 21 Henry VII [1505]. Condition : The said Richard Crosse to have peaceable occupation of lands and burgages in War'tre and Liverpool, conveyed to him by the said Sir John Ireland by a pair of Indentures of even date with the Bond.

No. 169. Litherland and Ford.

1505/6. Grant from William Davy to Richard Crosse, of Lyverpull, Esq., and Hugh Raynforth, chaplain, of all his messuages, tenements, &c., in Lydyrlond and ffordejuxta-Sefton, in the county of Lancaster : Attorns Roger Crosse to deliver seisin. Witnesses :

William Molyneux, Esq., William More, Esq., John Haydock, and others.

Given at Litherland the 6th of February, 21 Henry 7. [1505/6].

No. 170. Liverpool and Fazakerley.

1507. Grant from John Crosse, clerk, Rector of St. Nicholas in ffleche Shamollys, in London, to John fflecher, chaplain, John, son of Richard Crosse, Thomas, son of George Raynford, William More, and Evan Haghton, gent., Roger ffasakerley, and William Lake, of Lyrpole, their heirs and assigns, of all his lands, tenements, meadows, feedings, pastures, mill pond, woods, rents, &c., in Lyrpole, or elsewhere, in co. Lanc. He also gives to the same persons all the lands, tenements, &c., in

G

ffasakerley, which he holds by the feoffment of his relation, Hugh Botchyll, clerk ; also the premises bought of William Lyghtwodde in the same township. He makes this grant for the fulfilment of his last Will:

Dated 16th April, 22 Henry 7 [1507].

No. 171.
Walton-on-the-Hill and Adlington.

1509. Grant from Roger, son and heir of Richard Crosse, late of Lyverpole, to Richard Crosse, his father, for life, all his messuages, lands, tenements, &c., in Walton, near Lyverpole, and in Adlington, co. Lanc., which he inherited from Elizabeth, his mother, one of the daughters and heiresses of Roger Walton, late of Walton ; also all the messuages, lands, &c., which he had by the gift of his father. Remainder, after his father's death, to John Crosse, chaplain, his brother, for life ; Remainder to Robert, brother of John, and the heirs of his body lawfully begotten ; Remainder to Richard, brother of William, and his heirs and assigns for ever : John Coke to deliver seisin. Witnesses :

William Molyneux, Esq., William More, Esq., William Chorley, Nicholas Fazakyrley, Richard Standish, and others.

Given at Walton, on the 18th day of June, 1 Henry VIII [1509].

No. 171*.
Counterpart of No. 170.

No. 172.   *Tunstyd.*

1512. Beatrix, daughter and heiress of George Pemberton, to John Crosse, clerk, rector of All Saints', Turvey, co. Bedford.

Bond in one hundred pounds, payable at the Feast of St. John Baptist next.

Dated 15th November, 4 Henry VIII [1512].

Condition : She not to alienate or sell any lands, tenements, &c., belonging to her as one of the daughters and heiresses of George Pemberton, son of John Pemberton, late of Tunstyd, co. Lanc., gent., except to her own sisters and to her heirs, and only with the assent of said John Crosse, who hath borne charges for the recovery of the said premises from Hugh Pemberton, uncle of the said Beatrix.

No. 172*.
Counterpart of No. 172.

No. 173. *Liverpool.*

1513. Grant from Richard Crosse, of Chorley, gent., to William, his son, and Blanche and Margaret, his daughters, of one tenement in Le Chapell Strete, in Lyverpole, now in the occupation of Robert Sudale; one close in Lyverpole, in the occupation of Richard Dowse, and another close called the Middle Hey, now in the occupation of John Rose, and another close in the occupation of John Haydok; and twelve selions in Le Shrefe-acres, and five selions upon Le See Bonke; two selions upon Le See Bonke, in the occupation of Richard Plowmbe; For their joint lives and the life of the survivor of them; Remainder to the grantor: Robert Chorley to deliver seisin.

Dated 24th day of June, 5 Henry VIII [1513].

No. 174. *Liverpool.*

1514. Lease from Richard Crosse, of Lyverpole, "squyer," and Roger, his son and heir-apparent, to Adam Dandy, late of Lyverpole, for forty years from the Feast of St. Michael the Archangel next, of a parcel of ground in the Dale Strete in Lyverpole, lying between grounds of Thomas Secom on the east, and grounds belonging to the Altar of St. Nicholas, within the Chapel of St. Nicholas of Lyverpole, on the west, upon which the said Adam hath reared a house of three bays in length; paying yearly two pence at Michaelmas: The lessee to keep the house in tenantable repair: Power of distraint if the rent be in arrear for twelve days.

Given 20th day of August, 6 Henry VIII [1514].

Signatures of Ryẽ Crosse and Rog' Crosse. [In English.]

No. 174.*

Counterpart of No. 174.

No. 175. *Chorley.*

1515. Richard Crosse, of the co. of Lancaster, gentleman, to Roger Breres, yeoman and draper in the same county, Covenants on the Marriage of the said Roger with Blanche Crosse, daughter of the said Richard, which is to take place before Pentecost next: The said Roger is to receive twenty pounds of lawful money of England, at St. John Baptist and St. Martin in winter, at the hands of the said Richard.

Dated at Chorley the 6th day of May, 7 Henry VIII [1515]. [In English].

No. 176.   *Childwall and Walton.*

1519.   Decree of the Official of the Bishop of Chester, dissolving the Marriage of Letitia Norres, of Childwall parish, with Roger Crosse, of the parish of Walton, for want of consent, their parents having compulsorily espoused them when children.

Dated the 12th day of December, 1519.

[Partly frayed away].

No. 177.   *Barton-on-Irwell.*

1521.   John Bothe, Rector of Barton upon Yrwyll, to Laurence Asshow, gent.   Bond in forty pounds, payable at Pentecost.   Dated 8th day of May, 13 Henry VIII [1521].   Condition: The said John Bothe, before the Feast of the Translation of St. Thomas the Martyr next, to grant a lease to the said Laurence Asshow of the Tithe of Holme in Barton, in the co. of Lanc., which John Paslow, Abbot of Whalley, granted to Sir John Bothe, knt., father of the above bounden John Bothe, for certain years yet to come ; and to keep the said Laurence harmless in the enjoyment of the same, and to pay to the said Laurence seven marks before the Feast of the Nativity of St. John the Baptist next ensuing, and also all such sums of money as the said Laurence has paid and laid out for the use of the said John. [In English.]

Signature of Jno. Both.

No. 178.   *Liverpool, &c.*

1530.   Grant from John Crosse, clerk, Rector of Mulso, co. Bucks, to Sir Ewins Quykk, clerk, Geo. Goldwell and William Dowse, of all his lands, tenements, meadows, feedings, pastures, woods, &c., which were formerly held by John Crosse, his grandfather, in Lyverpole, Kyrkdale, Darby, Wartre, Holand, Heley, Knowseley, Wolton Magna, Wolton Parva, and Wigan, in the county of Lancaster, which came to him by inheritance after the death of Roger Crosse, his brother : Except all those messuages, lands, &c., which John Mordaunt, jun[r], and Edmund ffeteplace, esq[rs], Roger Hoggeson, and Henry Holyweil, held by his feoffment in Coppull, in co. Lanc., also a tenement in Heth Charnok, in the same county, as per charter dated 24th June, 20 Henry VIII, for the fulfilment of his last Will and Testament.   Attorns Humphrey Crosse, clerk,[1] and Richard Dowse, husbandman, to deliver seisin.

---

[1] Priest of the chantry of St. Katherine's, Liverpool.

Dated the 12th day of October, 22 Henry VIII [1530].
Small round seal of red wax : a stork proper.

No. 179. *Liverpool.*

1533. James Crosse, gent., brother and heir of John Crosse,
clerk, deceased, William Westby, and James Wynstanley,
to Roger Breres, George Garstan, yeoman, Blanche,
wife of Roger Breres, and Margaret, wife of George
Garstan, sisters of said John Crosse : Bond in four
hundred marks, payable on St. John Baptist's day next.
Dated 4th April, 24 Henry VIII [1533].

Condition : To keep and perform the Award of Lau-
rence Ireland and Laurence Asshow on behalf of James
Crosse, and of Thomas Bulkeley, clerke, parson of
Brynhill, and of Robert Swansey, on behalf of Roger
and George, concerning the messuages, lands, &c.,
which belonged to John Crosse, Richard Crosse, and
John Crosse, clerk, son and heir of Richard, all deceased :
The Award to be made with the assent of Henry
Farington and Roger Asshowe.

Signature of James Crosse.

No. 180. *Liverpool.*

1532/3. James Wynstanley, Laurence Ireland, and Laurence
Asshowe, complainants, against Roger Breres, and
Blanche, his wife, and George Garstan, and Margaret,
his wife, defendants.

Final Concord concerning 16 messuages, 200 acres
of land, 10 of meadow, 300 of pasture, 20 of wood,
300 of heath and furze, and 10 shillings rent in
Lyverpole, Magna Wolton, [West] Darby, Wartre, Everton, Coppul, Guilborn, Heth Charnok, and Kirkdale,
lately held by Edward Crosse, William Dowse, and
Johanna, late wife of William Crosse deceased, for their
lives, being the heritage of the aforesaid Blanche and
Margaret : And for this Fine and Release the said
Laurence, James, and Laurence gave to Roger, Blanche,
George, and Margaret, one hundred pounds.

Dated at Lancaster, Monday, 5th week of Lent,
25 Henry VIII [1532-3].

No. 181. *Liverpool.*

1534. Deed Poll, whereby James Crosse, citizen and goldsmith
of London, acknowledges the receipt, from Roger
Asshawe, of the co. of Lancaster, Esq., of £9 6s. 8d.,
in full satisfaction of one hundred marks sterling in

accordance with an Indenture of Covenants made on the marriage of John Crosse, son and heir of the said James, with Alice, daughter of the said Roger, as per Indenture dated 11th October, 25 Henry VIII.

Dated the 17th day of November, 26 Henry VIII [1534].   Signed p me James Crosse.

No. 182.   *Liverpool: Crosse Hall,*

1538.   Grant from Johanna Crosse, widow, relict of William Crosse, brother and heir of John Crosse, clerk, deceased, to James Anderton, gen', and Christopher Hogh, gen', of that capital messuage, called Crosse Hall, with lands and tenements adjoining, in Lyverpole; also all the lands, &c., which she had in the fields of Lyverpole, and Walton near Lyverpole, for the term of her life, on condition that the said James and Christopher shall before Easter next, re-convey the said capital messuage to her for life.

Dated 1st March, 29 Henry VIII [1538].

No. 183.   *Liverpool.*

1538.   Grant by James Anderton. Christopher Hogh, Thomas Banastre, chaplain, and Thomas, son of Rich. Banastre, Esq., to Johanna Crosse, widow of William Crosse, brother and heir of John Crosse, clerk, deceased, of the capital messuage called Crosse Hall, in Lyverpole, and lands in the fields of Lyverpole and Walton, which they hold by the feoffment of the said Johanna Crosse, for her life. They attorn Thomas Walbank and Thomas Ball to deliver seisin.

Dated 14th day of April, 29 Henry VIII [1538].

No. 184.   *Liverpool, &c.*

1538.   Roger Ashowe, esq., and Laurence Asshowe, gent., complainants, against James Crosse, defendant.

Final Concord at Lancaster, concerning 25 messuages, 300 acres of land, 40 of meadow, 200 of pasture, 10 of wood, 300 of heath and furze, 100 of turbary, and 10⁵ rent, in Lyverpole, Everton, Magna Wolton, Parva Wolton, [West] Derby, Coppull, Heth Chernok, Wygan, and Golbourn.   For this concession and fine the said Roger and Laurence paid to the said James one hundred pounds sterling.

No. 184*.
Counterpart of No. 184.

No. 185. *Heath Charnock.*

1538. James Crosse, citizen and goldsmith of London, to Roger Asshawe, of Heth Charnok, in co. Lanc.

Bond in three hundred pounds sterling, payable at Christmas : If not paid, to be subject to Statute Staple. Dated 19th day of November, 30 Henry VIII [1538]. [No condition.] Signature : p me Jamyes Crosse.

Three seals of red wax : on one a Tudor rose beneath a royal crown ; another shows the Crosse crest, a stork proper ; the third is an impression of an antique gem.

No. 186. *Liverpool.*

1539. The rent of Lyûpole due at the Annũciacion last past payed by Rob't Mosse vnto Laur' Asshowe, xx^th day of Aprill Anno tricẽsio Henr' octaui.

In p'ms of John Edmñdson - - - - -	x^s	
I^p for the Mylne xi^s viii^d vnde Dño Regi et sic recepi - - - iij^d		
I^p Robt Mosse for betenhey - - - - -	x^s	
I^p Thõs Dowse - - - - - - - - -	iiij^s	ix^d
Idm Thomas for Wod'hey - - - - -	iij^s	
Vx' Henr' Colne for hyr pt of the howse -		
I^p John Barker for his part - - - - -		xxj^d
Margaret Crosseby for hyr howse - - -		ij^d
Vx' Edwarde Shirelakers - - - - -		xv^d
John Valentine - - - - - - - -		xvj^d
Elsabeth Barker - - - - - - - -		xv^d
Vx' Brodeheyde - - - - - - - -	ij^s	vj^d
Robt Asspes for ffysshe yords - - - -		xvj^d
Elsabeth Dike - - - - - - - - -	ij^s	vj^d

Sm̃, xlij^s iij^d

I^p payed by the said Robt to the said Laur' the arrerage of Michaelmas rent left due in the tyme of James Crosse - xij^s
Whereof the said Laur' delyuf to the said Robt for the burde of Thõs. Crosse due afor Andrews day last - - - - - - iij^s
And the residue of the said xii^s is in the hands of the said Laur' to pay to the said James.

M^d Delyuf by the said Laur' to the said Robf for the burde of the said Thomas Scole hyr and Capp syth Andrews day last - - - - - - - - - - - - - x^s
I^p deliûf to the said Robt for his labor - ij^s

Et remanet Clare xxix^s v^d

M^d receyued from Robt Mosse by the
hands of Wiłłm Dowse at Manchesr
payed to the hands of my brothr Laur'
the xxv^th day of Octobr A° tricēsio p̃mo
Henr' octaui of the Michaelmas Rents
of Lyũpole due last past - - - - ·   v.

[On paper, side frayed.]

No. 187.   *London.*

1545. Nicholas Mighell, of London, beer-brewer, to James
Crosse, citizen and goldsmith, of London : Quitclaim
of all actions and demands, by reason of a bond of the
said James. [No particulars given.]

Dated 4th day of December, 37 Henry VIII [1545].

Signature : p me Nychlin Mighell.

No. 188.   *Liverpool.*

1560. John Crosse, of Lyverpole, Esq., to Ralph Egecar and
Elizabeth, his wife, and Thomas and Martyn, sons of
the late Peter Rymor. Lease, in consideration of seven
pounds, for twenty-one years, of a messuage in Le Dale
Strete in Lyverpole, late in the occupation of Peter
Rymor, deceased. Lessees to pay sixteen shillings
yearly, and not to sub-let.

Sealed in the presence of William Lawrence, Thomas
Toxtaffe, John Durnyng, Giles Rygbie, and Adam
Pendylton.

Dated 21st of May, 2 Elizabeth [1560].

No. 189.   *Liverpool.*

1561. William Chorley, of Chorley, Esq., to John Crosse, of
Lyverpole, Esq. Bond in three hundred pounds,
payable at Michaelmas.

Dated 12th of August, 3 Elizabeth [1561].

Condition : To observe the covenants in certain
indentures of bargain and sale of the same date.

No. 190.   *Walton and Fazakerley.*

1561. William Chorley, of Chorley, Esq., to John Crosse, of
Lyverpole, Esq. Confirmation of certain Indentures
dated 12th of August, 3 Elizabeth [1561], whereby
certain lands in the hamlets of Walton and Fazakerley
are conveyed, viz. : Denton's house, Tentors Hey,
Sponne Hey, the Two Acre, the Barn Croft, the Over
East Field, the Myddle Shott, the Laugher Acre, the
Preyste Meadow, and Brande-Yarth, now in the tenure
of William Chorley, the Round Hey, the Pykell, the

Gorsye Croft, being part of a large close called Gorsy Hey, with access for waggons and carriages. Brandearth is reserved to William Chorley and his heirs as tenants and farmers. Giles Rigbye and William Secum attorned to deliver seisin.

Dated 20th of September, 3 Elizabeth [1561].

No. 191. *Liverpool.*

1562/3. John More, of Banck House, near Liverpole, Esq., to John Crosse, of Lyverpole, Esq. Bond in forty pounds, payable at Lady Day. Dated 25th of February, 5 Elizabeth [1562-3]

Condition: To abide and observe the award of the following arbitrators, viz.: Richard Fazakerley, Thomas Bastwell, and Alderman Robert Corbet, all of Lyverpole, on behalf of John More, and John Maynwaring, of Liverpole, merchant, John Jolie, of Leigh, yeoman, and Laurence Breres, of Up-Walton, gent., on behalf of John Crosse, concerning the division of certain parcels of land in a close, croft, or hey in the Dale Strete, called Asshe Heyghe : The Award to be made in writing before Lady Day.

No. 192. *Heley.*

1563. John Crosse, of Lyverpole, to Robert Worsley, of Anglezark, and Margaret, his wife. Lease of a messuage and tenement in Heyghley, co. Lanc., in the occupation of James Crompton, for the term of their lives, in consideration of £10 and a yearly rent of twenty shillings.

Sealed in the presence of Roger Brodehurst, John Nyghtingale, and Richard Brown.

Dated 20th of July, 1563.

No. 193. *Liverpool.*

1564. Robert Fazakerley of [West] Derbye, gent., to John Crosse, of Lyverpole, Esq. Conveyance of a close of land called Pryor's Hey, in Lyverpole, formerly belonging to the Monastery of Byrkenhead, and by Letters Patent of Philip and Mary granted to Edmund Moyses, of London, haberdasher, Richard Bourstall and Richard Forster, yeomen, and by them sold on the 23rd of November, 4 and 5 Philip and Mary, to William, son and heir of Sir Richard Molyneux, Knight, who sold the same on the 6th of April, 1 Elizabeth, to the said Robert Fazakerley.

Present at the sealing thereof, William Secum, Richard Longworth, and Ralph Wynstanley.

Dated 18th of April, 6 Elizabeth [1564]. [In English].

H

1564.   Robert Fazakerley to John Crosse.   Grant of the Pryor's
         Hey. [Same as No. 193. In Latin.] Richard Abraham,
         attorney, delivered seisin thereof on 29th of April,
         6 Elizabeth [1564].

1564.   John Crosse, of Lyverpole, Esq., to Thomas Roose,
         senior, of Lyverpole.   Grant of a parcel of land in Le
         Eastham Dale, in Lyverpole Field, bounded on the east
         by land of John Mosse, late of Everton, deceased, now
         in the tenure of William Fletcher and Elizabeth Walsh,
         widow; on the south by land of John More, Esq., in
         the occupation of Laurence Heyghe; on the west by
         land of Henry Tarleton, lately deceased; and on the
         north by lands late of the Chantry of St. John, in the
         tenure of Thomas Roose, senior.   Rendering yearly
         one red rose on St. John Baptist's Day.   Nicholas
         Tomasson and James Melling attorned to deliver seisin.
         Dated 21st of June, 1564.

1564.   Deed Poll, whereby John Crosse, of the Queen's majesty's
         borow of Liverpole and port-town in her highnes Royal
         Realme of England, Esquier and Marchaunte, consti-
         tutes Christopher Crosse, his natural legitimate brother,
         his undoubted attorney, to buy and sell in the realme
         of " Hispayne " forty tons of iron and trayne [oil], &c.
              Given on 4th of July, 1564, at Lyverpole, per
         Pendilton, Recordat'.

1569.   Thomas Herdman, of Warrington, paver, to John Crosse,
         of Lyverpole, Esq.   Bond in forty shillings, dated 7th
         of September, 11 Elizabeth [1569].   Condition: To
         uphold the paving of one part of the Dale Strete in
         Lyverpole for one year, and of another part for two
         years.

1574/5. Thomas Bytaughe, of Dublin, to John Crosse, of Lyver-
         pole, gent.   Bond in forty pounds, dated 13th of January,
         7 Elizabeth [1574-5].   Condition: To deliver unto John
         Crosse true and perfect copies of the licence granted
         by the Queen for the transportation of yarne out of
         Ireland, under the hand and seals of the Lord Keeper
         of Ireland, the Mayor of Dublin, and three Aldermen,
         before 8th of March next.

No. 199. *Liverpool.*

1575. Richard Foxe, of Manchester, merchant, to John Crosse, of Lyverpole, gent. Bond and acknowledgment of a debt of forty shillings due and to be paid to John Crosse. [No condition.]

Sealed 22nd of April, 17 Elizabeth [1575].

No. 200. *Liverpool.*

1574. Thomas Dawber, of Bootle, smith, to William Longworth, of Lynacre, and Robert Webster, of Ayntree. Grant (reciting a previous agreement as to the premises between Thomas Dawber and Bryan Webster, dated 12th of May, 16 Elizabeth) of a quarter of a burgage, with houses and buildings, in Chapel Strete, Lyverpole, in the tenure of George Ferror, to the use of Thomas Dawber and Margaret his wife for life, then to the use of John Matherer (base son of Elizabeth Matherer deceased) and Katherine Webster, daughter of Brian Webster (which Katherine the said John had to wife), for their lives, remainder to their heirs, remainder to the right heirs of the grantor: William Golborne attorned to deliver seisin.

Dated 17th of May, 16 Elizabeth [1574].

No. 201. *Woolton Magna.*

1577. John Crosse, of Lyverpole, to Robert Pemberton. of Woolton Magna, husbandman, and Ellyn, his wife. Lease for their lives of one messuage, or tenement, in Much Woolton, at a yearly rent of ten shillings. Lessees to repair, sustain, and maintain premises, and make them defensable against wind and rain.

Sealed 4th of May, 19 Elizabeth [1577], in presence of Anthony Lunt.

No. 202. *Liverpool.*

1578. Thomas Secome, of Lyverpole, gent.. to John Poley, of Melling, gent. Marriage covenants, whereby it is agreed that Rauff, son and heir apparent of Thomas Secome. is to marry Catherine, daughter of John Poley, before the 18th of November next; Thomas Secome is to settle on Cathcrine one capital messuage, in the Dale Strete, in Lyverpole, now in his own occupation, with lands on the backside thereof, now in the occupation of Myles Lyptrotte; also three butts, or lands, in the Town Field, viz. : one in the Gallow Field, another in Higher Heyvielands, and the other in the Lower Heyvielands; also herbage for two cows in the Gorsty Field; To the

H 2

use of the said Catherine, or to Richard Jollybrand and James Botyll, for her life, as her jointure; Thomas is to occupy the premises for one year, paying one pepper corn; Thomas is to find Rauff and Catherine with meat, drink, clothes, lodging, and other necessaries for bed and board, and one comely chamber, with a chimney; If desired, Thomas will convey the estate to Robert Corbet and Rauff Burscoughe for her jointure; John Poley is to pay £60 to Thomas Secome, at the Chapel of Melling, also to Rauff and Catherine £10 at the house of John Poley, and Thomas is to pay £10 at same place in the year 1579; Each binds himself in 200 marks to complete the contract.

Given the 4th of October, 20 Elizabeth [1578]. Witnesses: Rauff Burscogh, John Crosse, Thomas Bavand, Robert Corbett.

No. 203. *Liverpool.*

1579/80. John Wanton, citizen and grocer, of London, to John Crosse, of Lyverpoole, gent. General release of all claims, actions, &c., to 25th of November last.

Sealed in presence of Tho. Lucas, servant to Robert Preston, and John Russell.

Dated 2nd of February, 21 Elizabeth [1579/80].

No. 204. *Woodchurch.*

s. d. Yearly Rents of lands sold unto my "Lord of Darby," in c. 1580. Woodchurch and Knoctorum, in the County of Chester, viz.:—Woodchurch: Lawrence Pemberton, 33ˢ 4ᵈ; William Coventry, 15ˢ 4ᵈ; William Wersewell, 2ˢ 4ᵈ; chief rent 4ˢ; Wood in Woodchurch, 0; sūm is 56ˢ. Knoctorum: Robert Chantrell, 30ˢ 11ᵈ; John Bird, 30ˢ 11ᵈ; Richard Coventry, 30ˢ 11ᵈ. The Old Wood, 10ˢ. Knoctorum Wood 0. Sūm is 6ˡⁱ 2ˢ 9ᵈ.

No. 205. *Liverpool.*

1582/3. Thomas Rose, of Liverpoole, husbandman, to John Crosse, of Liverpole. Grant of a parcel of land in Eastham Dale, in Liverpoole, which Thomas lately had of the grant of John Crosse, deceased, father of the above John Crosse.

Dated 6th of March, 25 Elizabeth [1582/3]. Witnesses:

George Rainforth, Roger Rosse, Thomas Rosse, and John Thomason. Seisin witnessed by George Rainforth, John Thomas, Roger Rosse, and Thomas Caly.

Dated 6th March, 25 Elizabeth [1582/3].

No. 206. *Liverpool.*

1582/3. Thomas Rose to John Crosse. Bond in £10 dated 6th March, 25 Elizabeth [1582-3].

Condition : To hold and keep indemnified certain parcels of land in Easthamdale which the said Thomas Rose had of John Crosse, father of the said John Crosse party hereto. Witnesses : Geo. Raynforth, John Thomas, Roger Rosse, and Thomas Rosse.

No. 207. *Noctorum.*

1624. John Crosse, of Liuerpoole, Esq., to Thomas Coventry, of Knocktorum, yeoman. Lease for 3 lives, being those of Richard and William his sons and Ann his daur., of lands in Knocktorum, in consideration of £100 and a yearly rent of £1 14s. 3d. Witnesses : William Banister, John Chantrell, William Chantrell, and William Felles, clerk.

Dated 2nd February, 1624.

No. 208. *Fazakerley.*

1637. Ralph Seacome, jun., son and heir of John Seacome, deceased, to John Crosse, of Liverpool, Esq. Grant, in consideration of £26 13 4, of certain lands in Fazakerley, called Smyth's field, Dobbs' field, Gorstey Worral, &c. John Banks and Edward Turner attorned to give possession. Witnesses :

John Foxe, James Hourocks, Ralph Winstanley, Richard Carr, Richard Cropper, of Walton, Ellis, son of Ralph Bridge, and Robert Mercer.

Dated 12th of June, 1637.

No. 209.

Copy of the Rental of the Estates taken on the death of John Crosse, Esq., who died 3 October, 1640, leaving his son Richard his next heir, aged 16 years 3 months and 3 days. Taken at Preston, 30th of April, 17 Charles I [1641].

Liverpool.

Thirty messuages and burgages, 1 dovehouse, 1 windmill, 60 acres of meadow, 40 of pasture, and one of wood, with appurtenances in Leverpoole, held of the King, as of his Duchy of Lancaster, in free burgage by 23s 10d yearly rent, worth by the Feodary's certificate - £4 0 0

Parcels of land in Liverpool Town field - - - 20s

Chorley and Helay.

One messuage called Crosse Hall, 40 acres of land, 5 of meadow, 30 of pasture, and 40 of wood, in Chorley, holden of the Rt. Hon. William, Earl of Derby, in soccage, as of the late dissolved monastery of St. John of Jerusalem, by 4^d rent, worth 5^s; premises in Helagh, in Chorley, held of Richard Sherburne and Alexander Rigby, Esq^{rs}, as of their Manor of Chorley, in soccage by rent of 24^c 8^d, and worth £3 6 8 by Feodary's certificate - - - - - - - - - - - - £2 6 8

The residue of the premises in Heley and Chorley - - - - - - - - - - - - - £1 5

Mellor and Showley.

Eight messuages, 200 acres of land, meadow, and pasture in Mellor and Showley. Those in Mellor are held of that manor in free soccage, and worth -   25^s

Of those in Showley the tenure is not known, but are worth - - - - - - - - - - - - -   20^s

Goosnargh.

Eight messuages and 100 acres of land, meadow and pasture in Goosnargh, held of the King, as of his Duchy of Lancaster, by knight service; worth -   40^s

Walton and Fazakerley.

Two messuages and 50 acres of land, meadow and pasture, in Walton and Fazakerley, next Leverpoole, holden of William Earl of Derby, in soccage by fealty; worth   10^s

West Derby, Everton and Wavertree.

One messuage and 10 acres of land, meadow and pasture in West Derby, Everton and Wavertree, holden of the King as of his manor of West Derby, in soccage, by fealty, and 2^d yearly rent; worth - - - -   5^s

Coppull.

One cottage 1 acre of land in Coppull, holden of Will. Worthington, in soccage; worth - - - - -   6^d

Bretherton.

One windmill, 4 messuages, 50 acres of land, meadow and pasture in Bretherton, holden of the King as of his Duchy of Lanc. by knight service by $\frac{1}{200}$th part of a knight's fee; worth - - - - - - - - -   20^s

Com Cestr.

Woodchurch and Noctorum.

Eight messuages, 100 acres of land, 40 acres of meadow, 80 acres of pasture, 10 acres of wood, 100 acres of moor and turbary, in Woodchurch and Knocktorum, and a yearly rent of 4ˢ issuing out of lands in Knocktorum and Woodchurch, late in the tenure of Thomas Rice, holden of the King as of his manor of East Greenwich, in soccage; worth - - - - - - - - - 20ˢ

Sum £15 7 2; and thereof to his Maᵗʸ the part of 10ᵗʰ parcells amount to £9 6 0, and also the eleventh part of the ward's mother's lands valued at 20ˢ.

No. 210ª. *Heley.*

1624/5. William Tootell, of Heley, to John Crosse, of Crosse Hall, in Chorley, Esq. Grant of a moiety of a water mill, in Heley. Witnesses :
Richard Chorley, Thomas Gillibrand, Laurence Breres, William Worshed, and Ralph Winstanley.
Dated 28th January, 22 James I [1624/5].

No. 210ᵇ. *Healey.*

1651. Rich. Crosse, of Crosse Hall, in Chorley, Esq., to Richard Grey, of Haskine, yeoman. Grant of a messuage and lands, formerly Pollard's, in Healey, for £230. Witnesses :
Hugh Dickonson, Edward Farnworth, Laurence Breares, and Robert Baldwine.
Dated 5th of December, 1651.

No. 210ᶜ. *Healey.*

1655/6. John Tootell, of Healey, to Richard Crosse, of Crosse-hall, Esq. Quit-claim of Pollard's lands in Healey, for £4 . 8 . 6.
Dated 9th of March, 1655/6.

No. 210ᵈ. *Heley.*

1671/2. Richard Grey, of Healey, gent., to John Crosse, Esq. Grant of a messuage called Pollard's house and 46 acres of land in Heley, in consideration of £400 and a yearly rent of 1ˡⁱ 1ˢ 6ᵈ, to John Tootell : Fine on death 21ˡⁱ 10ˢ 0ᵈ. Witnesses :

Ri. Standish, Edw. Wall, Ra. Longworth, Thomas Allanson, William Moody, John Asbey, and Arthur Davis.

Dated 27th of February, 1671/2.

Produced at Duxbury, 28th of October, 1674, before Tho. Robinson, Nich. Rigbye, Ed. Dicconson, and Jo. Cockshutt, Commissioners.

No. 211.   Chorley.

1656. Richard Grey, plaintiff, against Richard Crosse, Esq., and Elizabeth his wife, and Robert Leigh, deforciants. Final Concord concerning 1 messuage, 1 barn, 15 acres of land, 10 of meadow, and 15 of pasture in Chorley. For this fine Richard Grey hath given £100 sterling.

Dated 27th of May, 1656.

No. 212.   Liverpool.

1677. The Mayor (Robert Williamson, Esq.), Bailiffs (William Travers and James Prescot, gentlemen), and Burgesses of the town of Liverpoole, to John Crosse, of Liverpoole, Esq. Grant of all the special enlargement of ground into the wastes of Liverpoole for uniformity of the north east end of Dale Street, and the buildings set out there, in consideration of an annual rent of ten shillings for one thousand years, issuing out of a certain burgage in Liverpoole known as the Whyt-Lyon, granted to them by the said John Crosse.

Sealed and delivered under the common seal of Liverpoole. Witnesses :

Robert Forster, Hamlet Carter, and James Hodgson.

No. 213.   Liverpool.

1681. John, son and heir of Richard Crosse, Esq., deceased, and Ann (daughter of Samuel Yate, clerk), wife of the said John, to Samuel Yate, clerk, and Peter and Thomas Yate. Marriage settlement of John Crosse with Ann Yate, whose portion was £400. The capital messuage in Liverpool called Crosse Hall, with lands belonging thereto, and lands in Chorley, Healey, Goosnargh, Longton, Derby, Everton, Wavertree, and Walton are settled in trust to pay to Ann, the wife, after the death of her husband John Crosse, and during the joint lives of Ann and of Frances, grandmother of John (viz., Frances Woolfall), an annuity of £60 per annum for her life, and a further sum of £60 a year after the death of both John and Frances, in lieu of dower; power to raise £1000 for younger children's portions; remainder to Thomas Crosse, eldest son of John and Ann, and other their sons in tail male.

Dated 10th of April, 1681.

No. 214. *Liverpool.*

1697. Thomas, eldest son of John Crosse, to Thomas Henshaw. Lease for three lives and 21 years of Crosse Hall and a messuage adjoining, the Scones Croft and meadow, the Middle Field, the bottom of the North Hey, and the Deal Croft in the Town Field, in Liverpool; to hold during the lives of Radcliffe Henshaw, his wife, and John and Thomas, their sons, and 21 years after the death of the survivor of them, at the yearly rent of 20 shillings.

Dated 26th of February, 1697.

No. 215. *Liverpool.*

1698. Thomas Crosse and Mary (Clayton) his wife, to Richard Brook, Thomas and William Clayton, and Richard Longworth. Settlement after the marriage of Thomas Crosse with Mary, grand-daughter of Thomas Clayton, of Adlington, in the parish of Standish. Her jointure to be £50 a year; Crosse Hall and lands in Liverpool settled to secure the same. Power to grant leases for three lives and 21 years; and to raise £1000 for younger children.

Dated 22nd of July, 1698.

No. 216. *Liverpool.*

1698. Chirograph of a fine levied by Thomas Crosse, at Lancaster, 26th of March, 1698, of Crosse Hall and other lands in Liverpool, comprised in the Marriage Settlement of 10th April, 1681. [No. 213].

No. 217. *Liverpool.*

1709. Thomas Jackson, of Little Eccleston, admin^r of Peter Yate, to Richard Clayton, of Adlington. The estates, in Liverpool and elsewhere, settled in April, 1681, are granted to Richard Clayton, in order to raise £726.13.4 for the children of John Crosse, dec^d, viz.: Thomas and John, and five daughters, "all unpreferred at his death."

Dated 2nd of May, 1709.

1724. Richard Clayton, Richard Crosse, and others, to Robert Leigh, of Chorley. Assignment of the remainder of the term of 99 years of the settlement of 1681, unto Robt. Leigh in consideration of £726 . 5 . 0. Dated 14th of February, 1724.

1726. Richard Crosse and Ann (Legh) his wife, against Wrightington Woosey, Rich. Woosey, and others. Deed for suffering a Recovery of Crosse Hall and demesne, in Liverpool, and Crosse Hall and demesne, in Chorley, with other lands : The Recovery to enure to the use of the said Richard Crosse. Dated 15th and 16th of March, 1726.

1727. A common Recovery of lands, &c., in Liverpool, Chorley, &c. suffered at Lancaster 25th of March, 1727.

1727. Robert Leigh, Richard Crosse, and others, to Sir Thomas Standish, of Duxbury, Bart., and Richard Houghton, merchant. Assignment of the remainder of a term of 99 years in certain messuages and lands in Liverpool, in consideration of the sum of £726 . 5 . 0, with consent of Robert Whitfield and others. Dated 22nd of November, 1727.

1736. Richard Crosse, James Hartley, and Will. Hawkshead, to Thomas Starkie. Mortgage of certain lands to secure £100 and £400. Dated 20th and 21st of December, 1736.

1742. Copy of Will of Richard Crosse, of Crosse Hall, in Chorley. Bequeaths Crosse Hall, in Liverpool, to Ann [Legh], his wife, James Hartley and Wm. White, of Manchester ; In trust to the use of his three sons and three daughters ; Charges his estate with £30 a year for his wife for life, and with £1000 for the portions of his five younger children. Dated 18th of November, 1742.

The following documents have only recently been placed in the Muniment room at Shaw Hill, having been bought from a dealer at Colchester, and given to Colonel Crosse by R. D. Radcliffe, in 1889:—

No. 224.

Wigan, Liverpool, West Derby.

1566. Indenture of Marriage Covenants between John Crosse,
7 Aug. of Liverpool, and John More, of Bancke-house, for a marriage between John Crosse (son and heir apparent of the said John Crosse) and Alice More (daughter of the said John More. John Crosse agrees to make an estate of the clear yearly value of £10 [see schedule] vnto George Ireland, of Hutte, Edward Tarbock, of Tarbock, John Harrington, of Huyton Hey, and William More (son and heir apparent of the said John More) to the use of Alice More for life : and John More promiseth to pay to John Crosse £150 by instalments, viz., £40 at the wedding, £30 at the following Pentecost, the balance by yearly instalments of £20. Witnesses :

George Ireland, Thomas Oldershaw, and Hamnet Dychefeld.

SCHEDULE.

In this Scedule Indented is conteyned all the mesuages landes and teñtes withe thappurteñnts geven and graunted in this Indenture herevnto annexed as hereafter ffollowethe

Lands in *Wegan.*

Inprimis one teñte withe thappurteñnts in the ocupacõn of John Jollye of the yearelye value of   xiij^s   iiij^d

Item one other teñte withe thappurteñnts in the tenure or occupacõn of Gyles Rigbie of ye yerely value of . . . . xxj^s

Item one other teñte withe thappurteñnts in the tenure or occupacõn of Alexander Buckley of ye value of . . . . . . xiiij^s

It. one teñte wth thapp^rteñnts in the tenure or occupacõn of Roberte Barrowe of the yearly value of   xij^s   viij^d

Item one teñte wth thapp^rtñnts in the tenure of Willm Burge of the yearely value of . . x^s   iiij^d

Item one teñte in the occupacõn of the wyffe of Willm Pembton of the yearely value of. . ix^s

Item a pcell of lande in the tenure or occupacōn
of Roḃte Whalley of the yearely value of . iijˢ iiijᵈ

It. one teñte with thappurteñnts in the occupacōn
of Xp̄ofer Gregson of the yearely value of . xˢ

It. a howse and garden in the tenure or occupacōn
of Thomas Barrowe of the yearely value of . iijˢ iiijᵈ

Item a howse and garden in the tenure or occupacōn of Thomas Laythwaite of the yearely
value of . . . . iiijˢ

It. lande laite in the holdinge of John Harryson of
the yearely value of . . . . . iiijˢ

Item one howse and garden in the tenure or occupacōn of Willm Byrche of the yearely value of iiijˢ

It. one barne and barne yorde in the tenure or occupacōn of Willm Skotte, of the yearely value of vjˢ

Item a pcell of grounde in the tenure or occupacōn
of Willm Langshawe of the yearely value of . xxᵈ

The Soñe of all the Landes in Wegan is vˡⁱ xvjˢ viijᵈ.
Due therof to the chyffe Lorde xjˢ ijᵈ

Landes in *Lyverpoll* and *Derbie.*

Inprimis a howse and garden, halffe an acre in Sal-
tanes More, one lande in the olde feyld and
three buttes in Estam Dayle, in the occupacōn
of Thomas Rose, of the yearely value of . vˢ viijᵈ

Item one teñte, two landes in the Overheuelande
one lande and a halffe in the Gallowe ffeilde
and halffe a land in Estam Dale in the occupacōn of Edmond Bancke of yᵉ yerely value of xˢ viiijᵈ

It. one howse and warehowse in thoccupacōn of
Thomas Wynstanley of the yearely value of . xᶜ

It. a howse and garden, one land in the Overheuelande and two buttes in the Gallowe ffeilde in
the tenure or occupacōn of Richarde Cropper
of the yearely value of . . . . . xˢ

Item David Allan two howses and yords of the
yearely value of . . . . . . vˢ

Item a howse and garden in the tenure or occupacōn of Willm Pendleton of yᵉ yearely value ijˢ vjᵈ

Item a howse in the tenure or occupacōn of John
Manwaringe of the yearely value of . . xiijˢ iiijᵈ

Item a howse and garden, one barne and barne
    yorde and one lande in the Stuttes in the
    tenure or occupacõn of Rawffe Egeker of the
    yearely value of .   .   .   .   .   . xxj^s x^d

It. a howse and garden in the tenure or occupacõn
    of the wyffe of Richard Dawber of ye value of iiij^s

Item a close in Derbie called Snodon in the tenure
    of Robte ffletcher of the yearely value of . xij^s

p me JHON CROSSE.

1570.   John Crosse's acknowledgment of the receipt from John
7 May. More of £10, being the last instalment of the £150,
    consideration of the marriage of his son John Crosse
    with Alice More.

INDEX.

The Figures in this Index refer to Nos. of Charters and not to Pages.

PLACES.

LIVERPOOL, WHEN NOT OTHERWISE SHEWN.

Adlington, 171

Banke-howse, 224
Barton-on-Irwell, 177
Berkeswell, 10
Bretherton, 209
Brockhurst 9
Burscogh, 129

Charnok-Richard, 52, 162
Childwall, 176
Chorley, 91, 94, 96, 116, 134, 140, 162, 175, 209, 211, 219
Coppull, 209
Craunton, 106, 112, 112a
Culcheth and Kenyon, 87, 89, 90, 93

Eccleshall, 99
Everton, 209

Fazakerley, 50, 170, 190, 208, 209
Flint, 53

Goosnargh, 209

Halewood, 49
Heath Charnok, 46, 185
Heley, 166, 192, 207, 209, 210, 211, 213
Holand, 165
Hutt, 224
Huyton, 163 ; Hey, 224

Ince (Wigan), 86

Kenyon, 66, 132, 143
Kirkdale, 100

Lathom, 5, 144
Legh, 75
Litherland and Ford, 169
London, 187
Lowton, 93

Mellor, 209

Noctorum, 207, 209

Ormskirk, 88

Parr, 119
Pemberton, 11a, 11b, 11c, 146
Preston, 84

Rivington, 47

Showley, 209
Solihull, 9
Speke, 162
St. Asaph, 145

Tarbock 224
Tunstyd, 172

Walton, 4, 50, 157, 171, 176, 190, 209
Wavertree, 158, 159, 160, 209
West Derby, 127, 161, 209, 224
Wigan, 6, 7, 12, 13, 14, 14*, 15, 17, 19-23, 23a, 23b, 23c, 23e, 25, 26, 27, 29, 30, 32, 34, 35, 36, 37, 38, 41, 43, 44, 45, 51, 57, 72, 73, 75, 76, 78, 79, 80, 82, 85, 95, 126, 138, 224
Woodchurch, 204, 209
Woolton, 201

NAMES.

f. *or* fil.=SON *or* DAUGHTER.

Abraham Ric., 194
Accres J., 50 ; Rog., 68
Adam (clerk) 18, (bailiff) 40, 42
——— le Cowper, 13
——— f. John, 30
——— f. Orm., 3, 8, 12, 23, 23a
——— f. Ric., 55, 58, 67, 68
——— f. Rob. (carpr.), 23, 32
——— f. Will., 18, 31, 33, 42
——— f. Will. f. Ra., 24, 28, 39

Adamson J. J., 139
Adlington Hugh, 162 ; Thos. f. Thos., 52 ; W., 47
Aikscogh Nic., 129
Alan le fuller, 14*, 23e, 27, 35
——— f. John, 24, 68
——— f. Walt., 14, 17, 25
Alex. f. Masse, 28
Aldous f. Elot, 31
Alice fil. Adam, 68
Alkmundebury W., 3

Allan David, 224
Allanson T., 210
Almaric le fuller, 25, 27, 35, 41
Altkar Ad., 33 ; Alice, 33 : John, 33
Alvandley Ric., 49
Amorison J., 56, 63, 64, 65, 66, 84 ; Ric., Nic., and Thurst., 66
Amundeville Ric., 10
Anderton Jas., 182, 183 ; Oliver, 140, 166 ; Rob., 116, 130 ; Thurst., 96, 113, 116, 130, 166
Anable f. W. Balle, 3
Annet Ra., 10
Asbey J., 210
Asshaw Ad., 15 ; Rich., 47 ; W., 47 ; W. f. Hugh, 47
Asshowe Alice, 181 ; Laur., 177, 179, 180, 184, 186 ; Rog., 181, 184, 185
Asshetou J., 130 ; W., 57
Ashton T., 93
Atherton H., 50, 119 ; Nich., 127 ; Sir W., 87
Aynesargh Ric., 55, 58, 59, 60, 61, 62, 63, 64, 67, 69, 70, 104 ; Ric. and Elene, 117
Aynsdale J., 33
Aynolfisdale Will. f. Rob., 18 ; Will. f. Ric., 18

Baker J., 23, 32
Baldwin Rob., 210
Balle Ad., 28 ; J., 83, 103 ; T., 83, 183 ; W., 1, 2
Banastre Hen., 36, 73 ; Ric., 183 ; Rog., 143 ; T. (chapl.), 183 ; W., 207
Banks Edm., 224 ; J., 84, 162, 208
Baret W., 42
Barker Ad., 98, 103
Baron Ad., 18, 40, 42 ; Elene, 24 ; Hen., 9 ; J., 62, 98 ; Ric., 1, 24, 28, 114 ; W., 1, 16, 39, 68
Barrowe Rob., 224 ; T., 224
Barri H., 10
Bastwell T., 191
Bavand T., 202
Baxter Rob., 57 ; Thurs., 78, 80
Bell J., 83, 118
Bellerby J., 163
Bendbow J., 99
Berkswell Ph., 10
Bikerstat Ra., 5
Birchover Ithel, 53
Bird J., 204 ; Rob., 99
Birkenhead Ad., 72, 73, 75, 76, 78, 80, 82, 85, 126 ; H., 126, 132, 147, 148, 148* ; J., 6, 13, 14, 14*, 17, 21, 22, 23*a*, 23*b*, 23*c*, 23*e*, 25, 27, 29, 32, 34, 41, 126, 130, 165 ; Ric., 148
Birom Hen., 126 ; T., 126
Blackburn Rob., 76
Blainscue J. and Dionisia, 9
Blake W., 69
Blakemore Ric., 4
Blaken Ric., 103
Blount W., 48
Blundell H., 130
Boghe Agnes, Alice, Hen., 34
Bold T., 123
Bolton Rob. f. Will., 43 ; W., 164
Bonell T., 128, 139, 141
Booth J. (rector), 177
Bootle Hugh, 123, 125, 128, 134, 135, 139, 170 ; Eleanor, 138 ; Jas., 202 ; Hen., 156 ; Tho., 135
Bothe J., 96
Botiller Ric., 127
Botling W., 6, 25
Botlinger W., 35, 38, 41 ; Ric., 44
Bowland Rob., 139
Bradshaw T., 91, 130 ; W., 14*, 17, 19
Breres Blanche, 179, 180 ; Laur., 191, 210 ; Rog., 175, 179, 180
Bretargh W., 106

Bretherton H., 113, 128, 139
Bridge Ellis, 208 ; Ra., 208
Brockhurst Alex., 9*b*
Broadhurst Rog,, 192
Brook Ric., 215
Brouneson Ad. f. Tho., 31
Brown J., 101 ; Ric., 192 ; W., 158, 159 : Gilb. f. W., 160
Buckley Alex., 224
Bulkeley Jas., 180 ; T., 180
Bulling Hugh, 7, 23
Bumble J., 84
Burge W., 224
Burgess Ric., 36 ; Rob., 160
Burgh Rob. f. Hen., 91, 94, 96
Burnhull Rob. f. Sr. T., 43, 44, 51
Burnul Peter, 11*c*
Burscogh Gilb., 147 ; Ric., 162, 202
Burstal Ric., 193
Burun Rob., 4
Bury Ra., 163 ; T., 163
Butler Ric., 127
Byrkenshaw Ad., 14
Bykerstath J., 117
Byrche W., 224
Byrum Hen., 130 ; T., 75
Bytaugh T., 198

Calson W., 162
Calvert J., 162
Caly T., 205
Cambayn Ad., 21
Carlill J., 162
Carnarvan Rog., 40
Carpenter A. f. Rob., 22, 23*a*, 23*b*, 23*c* ; Ric., 23*a* ; Tho., 22
Carr Ric., 208
Carter Hamlet, 212 ; Rog. 129
Carver Ric., 129
Castello W., 24
Caudray Rob., 108, 110, 113, 133, 134, 139 ; T., 113, 114, 117, 118
Chaloner J., 166 ; W. jun., 162 ; W. sen., 162
Chantrell J., 207 ; Rob., 204 ; W., 207
Charnok Edw., 94, 96
Charnock H., 52, 116
Chernok Rob., 162 ; Rog., 130, 139 ; T., 194
Child W., 59, 60, 61, 62, 63, 109, 110
Chisnall W., 95
Cholale Ad., 23*d*
Chorley Ric., 210 ; Rob., 173 ; W., 171, 189, 190
Chysenhale J., 37, 46 ; Rob., 46
Clapham Alice, 76
Clayton Alice, 41 ; Mary, 215 ; Ric., 217, 218 ; T. and W., 215
Cockshut J., 210
Coke Alice and Rog., 85 ; Will., 85, 138
Cokeyn J., 54, 105
Cole J., 92, 97, 98
Comyn Alex., 55
Cophull Ad., 21 ; J., 46, 47, 91, 94
Coppe Ric., 9
Corbet Rob., 191, 202
Corviser Ste. and Emma, 67
Cosin T., 80, 86
Coudray T, 83
Coupland J., 70
Coventry Ann, 207 ; Ric., 204, 207 ; T., 207 ; W., 204, 207
Craunton J., 106, 112
Crichelawe H., 162
Croft J., 73, 76, 78
Crompton Jas., 192
Cropper Ric., 208, 224

Crosse (Crucis) Adam, 7, 13, 20 ; Agnes, 165 ;
    Blanche, 175 ; Christopher, 196 ; Edmund,
    148, 148* ; Edward, 180 ; Elene, 13 ; Elizabeth,
    171 ; Hugh, 73. 75, 76, 78, 80, 126 ; Humphrey,
    178 ; James, 179, 181, 184, 185, 186, 187 ;
    Johanna, 182, 183 ; John, 3, 6, 11a, 11b, 14,
    14*, 17, 19, 20, 21, 22, 23e, 25, 26, 27, 29, 30,
    32, 34, 35, 36, 37, 38, 41, 142, 147, 148, 148*,
    149, 150, 151, 152, 153, 154, 156, 158, 159, 160,
    161, 164, 165, 167, 170, 171, 172, 178, 179, 181,
    182, 183, 188, 189, 190, 191, 192, 193, 194, 195,
    196, 197, 198, 199, 201, 202, 203, 205, 206, 207,
    208, 209, 210a, 210d, 212, 213, 214, 217, 224 ;
    Nicholas, 23e ; Richard, 20, 96, 97, 98, 101,
    107, 108, 109, 110, 112, 113, 116, 117, 118, 122,
    124, 125, 127, 128, 131, 133, 134, 135, 137, 138,
    139, 140, 141, 157, 163, 164, 166, 167, 168, 169,
    170, 171. 173, 174, 175, 179, 209, 210b, 210c,
    211, 213, 218, 219, 221, 222, 223 ; Robert, 121,
    171, 186 ; Roger, 169, 171, 174, 176, 178 ;
    Thomas, 186, 213, 214, 215, 216, 217 ; William,
    164, 167, 173, 180, 182, 183
Culchith Gilb., 26, 36

Daas W., 93
Dandy Ad., 174
Davenport J., 154
Davis Arthur, 210
Davy T., 84 ; W., 169
Dawber Marg., 199 ; Ric., 224 ; T., 199
Dawe del Bonk, 1
Delyot J., 100
Denbigh D., 104
Derby Lord, 204 ; Rob., 79, 82, 103, 110, 113, 114;
    Rob. and Eliz., 117 ; Rob. (M.), 118, 120, 121,
    123
—— William Earl of, 209
Dey Chr., 153 ; J., 92, 101, 102, 118, 123
Dickinson Edw., 210 ; Hamnet, 224 ; Hugh, 210 ;
    Rob., 95 ; T., 79
Ditchfield J., 49   [49
Ditton Ad., 103 ; J., 49 ; P., 109 ; Tho. f. Steph.,
Doudson J., 84
Doustes Ric., 49
Dowse Ric., 173, 178 ; W. 178, 179
Driffield J., 103
Durning J., 188
Duxbury J., 116, 130 ; T., 82, 85, 88, 95, 127
Dwerryhouse Ric., 142
Dychefeld Hamnet, 224
Dykeson W., 69

Eccles H., 4
Eccleston J., 70, 77 ; T. de, 6
Egecar Eliz., 188 ; Ra., 188, 224
Eldware W., 13
Ellison H., 159
Eltonhead J., 119
Eustace (draper) 67
Everton Gilb., 123
Eves T., 156
Ewys T., 161
Eyntre W., 4
Eyvys T., 164

Faber H., 23d, 23e ; Ran. f. Tho., 8 ; T., 1, 2
Fareclogh H., 105
Fairclogh Ric., 165
Farington H., 180 ; J., 74 ; Sir Rog., 105
Farnworth E., 210
Fazakerley Hen. f. Rob., 50 ; Ric. f. Ric., 50 ;
    Nic., 152, 154, 155, 158, 159, 160, 161, 171 ;
    W., 152, 154, 155, 161 ; Eliz. w. W., 161 ;
    Ric., 191 ; Rob., 193, 194 ; Rog., 170
Felles W. (clerk), 207

Ferror G., 199 ; J., 6, 30
Feteplace Edm., 178
Fitchling W., 90
Fleming Sir T., 91
Fletcher J., 170 ; Rob., 224 ; W., 195
Ford Ric., 141
Forester Ric., 193 ; Rob., 212
Formby J., 64, 65, 122 ; Margy., 67
Fourbourg Ad., 67
Foxe J., 80, 208 ; Nic., 55 ; Ric., 200 ; W., 24, 28, 4
Frekilton W., 12
Fulshaw H., 32, 34, 35, 36, 37, 38, 41, 43, 45, 51
    Hen., 20, 29, 30 ; Ric., 14*, 19, 20, 21, 23b
Fyncheden Sir W., 105

Galway Maur., 58
Garston G., 179, 180 ; Margt., 179, 180
Geoffrey f. Agnes, 1
—— f. Seyene, 2
Gernet J., 2
Gilbert (smith), 53
Gilibrond Ch. and Da., 129 ; Edm., 147 ; Gilb
    128 ; H., 43, 57 ; J., 23e ; J. and Eliz., 146
    Ric., 147, 202 ; T., 210 ; W., 37
Glest Rob., 162 ; T., 108, 118, 123, 125
Gogard Ad. f. Tho., 46 ; Ra. f. Will., 46
Goldwell G., 178
Gough J., 84
Green H., 89
Gregson Chr., 224
Grelle J., 49
Grey Ric., 210, 211, 213
Griffith D., 164

Haghe Hugh, 26, 36
Haghton Evan, 163, 170
Haighton T., 86
Halifax Ad., 20
Halliwell H., 178
Halshagh W., 31
Halsall Gilb., 5
Hanneknave Steph., 26
Harang H., 10
Haregue Ad., 53 ; Rog., 53
Harding T., 92
Harebron Hugh, 142, 149, 154 ; Jacob, 142 ; T., 15
    156
Harebrowne W., 164
Harrington Hamnet, 163 ; John, 224 ; Rog., 54
Harper Ric., 50 ; Rob., 59
Harrison J., 224
Hartley Jas., 222, 223
Hastelegh Hen., 6 ; Hugh, 6
Hawkshead W., 222
Haydok H., 54, 105 ; Sir H., 105 ; Hugh, 11, 1
    J., 169, 173
Hayle Jacob, 162
Henry (clerk) 11
—— (priest), 139
—— f. Holl, 6
Henshaw J., R., and T., 214
Henthorn J., 125
Herdman Matilda and Rob., 97 ; T., 197
Hey Laur., 195
Hibernia Ra., 1, 2 ; Ra. and Marj., 8
Highfield Rob., 25, 26, 32, 76
Hindley Ad., 23e ; T., 162 ; W., 162
Hitchcockson Rog., 52 ; Will, 52
Hodgson Jas., 212 ; Rog., 178
Hogh Chr., 182, 183 ; Edm., 162 ; Kath., 104, 11
    120, 125 ; John, 120, 121 ; Ric., 53 ; T., 104
Hoghton Sr. Ad., 74 ; Sr. Ric., 96
Holand J., 49 ; Rot. f. Rob., 11b, 11c ; Rob., 11
    Rog., 123 ; Sim f. Thurs., 11a, 11b ; Thur
    11c, 118 ; Sr., W., 12

olcroft T., 87 ; Thurst., 130
olt Jas., 93
opton J., 95
ornby Agnes. 37
oughton Ric., 221
ourocks Jas., 208
ugh (clerk), 17, 19, 20, 21, 22, 23*e*, 25, 27, 29, 30,
   32, 34, 35, 38, 41, 107
— (the dyer), 50
— fil. Rog., 23*a*
ull Ad., 46 ; J., 69, 70, 83, 97 ; Rog. f. Will., 14* ;
   W. f., 23*a*, 23*c*
ulm Ric., 83
ulton Rog., 86
uyton Jas., 158 ; Nic., 147

es Gilb., 45 ; Geo. f. Rog., 76 ; Hen., 14*, 86 ;
   Ric., 14*, 17, 23*e*, 36, 38, 41, 43 ; Ric and Ra.,
   76 ; Ric. f. Hugh, 76 ; Ric. (Wigan), 19, 23*e*,
   25, 29, 30 ; Rog., 76, 86 ; Will. f. Rog., 11*a*, 11*b*
eland Ad., 50 ; Geo., 224 ; J., 168 ; Laur., 179,
   180 ; Rob., 103
hel of Neston, 84

ackson T.. 89, 90, 217
enkinson H., 162
ewe W., 126
ohn (clerk), 39
— f. Ad. (clerk), of Liverpool, 61
— f. Ad. f. Sim., 62
— f. Almeric, 58, 59, 60, 61, 62
— f. Henr. and Alice, 5
— f. Hugh, 6, 19, 20, 21, 22, 25, 26, 27, 29, 32,
   34, 35, 36, 37, 38, 43, 45
— f. Hugh (mercer), 14, 14*
— f. Ra., 1
— f. Ric. f. Dob., 45
— f. Simon, 2
— f. Walt. (fuller), 41
— f. Will., 23*d*
— le Drawer, 106
— le Potter, 3
ohnson Hugh f. Hen., 84 ; J., 138
olie J., 191, 224

ay R. J., 59
elyng Sir Rob., 83
enian Jordan, 11*c*
ent T., 88
enteil Gilb., 10
enyon Ad. f. Math., 56, 66 ; Johanna, 134 ;
   Kath, 56, 66 ; Makin, 129 ; Math., 143 ; Will.,
   132
euerdale Rob., 51
ighley Sir Ric., 91
irkby J., 23*d*
irkdale Rob., 4 ; Sim., 83 ; W., 23*d*
Knife-smith Ad., 7
Kynarton Ric., 122
Kynknall Ad., 90 ; J., 87, 90, 93 ; J. and Em., 90 ;
   P., 87, 93

Lake Rob., 158, 159 ; W., 170
Lamare W., 10
Lamley J., 89, 90, 93, 106
Lancaster Earl Hen., 48
Langshaw W., 224
Lathom G. fil. Edm., 163 ; Rob. f. Rob., 5, 11*c*
Lawrence T., 162 ; W., 188
Lawton J. fil. Rob., 86
Layland Ad., 38 ; Matilda, 38
Laythwate T., 224
Leigh Rob., 211, 218, 221, 222
Lever Rog., 19, 20, 21, 22, 23*c*
Leyland Rog., 14

Lightwood W., 170
Liptrot Miles, 202
Lister Ric., 57
Liverpool Ad., 55 ; Ad. f. Ran., 16 ; Alice, 40 ;
   Corporation of, 212 ; Hugh de, 70, 81 ;
   John de, 134 ; John de, jun., 104, 121 ;
   Kath., 72, 77 ; Rob. Nich. de (clerk), 83,
   108, 118 ; Rob. (clerk), 68 ; Rob. f. Hen., 40 ;
   W. 40 ; W. (clerk) and Emma, 55 ; W. de, 54 ;
   W. (girdeler), 122 ; W. f. Ad., 58, 59, 60, 61,
   62, 63, 64, 67, 69, 74, 77, 104, 105, 125
Long Margy., 83
Longbak W. or J., 106
Longford Nic., 115
Longrow Ad., 55 ; Rob., 101, 102, 117
Longshaw J., 57 ; Ric., 82
Longton Elenor, 148, 148* ; Hen., 148, 148*
Longtre Gilb., 116 ; Ric., 140 ; T., 35
Longworth Ra., 210 ; Ric., 193, 215 ; W., 199
Lovel Sir J. and J., 91, 94 ; Matilda, 91, 94
Lucas T., 203
Lunt J., 92 ; W., 103, 139
Lydgate Rob., 64
Lynacre J., 81, 101-3, 110, 114, 117, 118, 128, 139 ; and
   Jelian, 139
Lyster W., 51, 82

Macclesfield Ric., 53
Manwaring J., 224
Mapleduram Ric., 16, 33
Marclan Ad. f. Ric., 13 ; H., 22, 34 ; Matt., 34
Mariotson Rog. f. Will., 67
Marsh Ad. fil. John, 51 ; H., 75, 76, 79, 84, 95 ;
   Hugh, 126 ; J., 36
Marshall Ad., 39 ; Hugh, 29 ; Ric. and Isabella,
   95
Matthew (clerk), 11*a*, 19
Mather Eliz., 199 ; J., 199
Matth. f. Ric., 33
Maykin, 132
Maynwaring J., 191
Melling Jas., 195
Mercer Hugh, 23*b*, 23*c* ; J., 163 ; Rob., 16, 208 ;
   Rog., 35 ; T., 162
Mercenarius Hugh, 7
Michael W., 162
Mighell Nic., 187
Milner H., 158
Moberley Matt., 12
Molyneux Agnes, 157 ; Rev. Jas., 157, 164 ; Laur.,
   157 ; Ric., 193 ; W., 169, 171, 193, 213
Moody Wm., 210
Morcote Walt., 10
Mordaunt J., jun., 178
More (Mora) Agnes, 2 ; Alice, 224 ; J., 2, 3, 8, 16,
   18, 23*d*, 24, 28, 31, 33, 39, 40, 42, 55, 68, 142,
   191, 195, 224 ; Margt., 104 ; Rand., 1, 2 ;
   Ric., 3, 16, 23*d*, 24, 28, 31, 33, 39, 40, 42, 68 ;
   Rob., 128, 149, 151, 153, 156 ; Rog. 85 ; T. 77,
   83, 92, 97, 98, 101, 102, 103 ; W., 39, 161, 169,
   170, 171, 224 ; Will. f. Rog., 60 ; W. f. T. 97
Morehouse J., 81, 92 ; Rob., 83, 118
Mosok H., 114, 125, 128, 134
Moss Eliz., 195 ; J., 195 ; Ric., 101, 102, 108
Mosse Rob., 156, 186
Moyses Edm., 193
Muckelfen H., 13
Multon W., 9
Munn Ric., 125
Myrescogh J., 88

Nayler W., 141
Nevin Rog., 95
Newport T., 55

Newcome Walt., 10
Nicholas (clerk), 12, 13, 58, 59, 60, 61, 62, 63, 69,
    70, 83, 98, 101, 102, 107, 108. 110, 113, 114
Nich. de Lyverpull (clerk). 118, 120, 121, 123
Nicholson W., 162
Nigel f. Hugh, 10
Nightingale J., 52, 192
Norris Alan, 5
Norreys H., 119 ; Letitia, 176

Occulshaw J., 86
Oldershaw T., 224
Oldenhale J., 10
Oldware W., 14
Osbaldeston J., 113, 114

Page Ric , 12, 29; T., 23c
Parbold W., 78
Parker Ric., 53
Parr Ric. 119; Hen , 71 : J., 71 ; Margt., 119 ;
    Ric., 119 ; Rob., 71
Paslew Abbot J., 177
Pasmyth J., 158, 160
Payn Simon, 43, 45, 51
Pemberton Ad., 11a, 11b, 19, 36, 37, 51 ;
    Aynhou, 11c ; Beatrice, 172 ; Ellen, 201 ;
    Geo., 172 ; Hen., 11a, 36 ; Hugh, 172 ; J. fil.
    Hugh, 146 ; Laur., 204 ; Roh., 201 ; Will., 224 ;
    Will. f. Ad., 11a, 11c.
Pendleton Ad., 188, 196 ; W., 224
Penereth W., 108, 118 ; W. and Cecilia, 83 ; T., 50
Peshal Ric., 99
Penulton T., 162 ; W., 162
Pierpoint Ric., 98 ; Rob., 15
Pilkington Ric., 15
Plombe H., 164 ; J., 158 ; Jacob, 162
Plumbe Ric., 173
Pole H., 53
Poley Cath., 202 ; J., 202
Potter J., 16
Prendergest Ric., 24
Prescot Jas., 212 ; J. fil. Rob., 51
Preston Rob., 152, 154, 203 ; W., 19
Prestwich Ra , 115

Quick Sir Ewin, 177

Radcliffe Christina, 11b, 11c; J., 115
Rainforth G., 205, 206 ; Hugh, 169 : T., 170
Redyth O., 115
Reeve Cecilia f. John f. Rich., 49
Ric f. Ad., 28
—— f. Ad. f. Grim., 19
— - - f. John f. Simon, 8
—— f. Michael, 19, 23a, 23b
—— f Ric., 3, 8, 31, 33, 39
—— f. Rob., 2
Richard (clerk), 23b, 37, 47
Ric de Fullers, 14
Rice Thomas, 209
Rich and Gilb. (mariners), 97; Gilb., 101, 102
Rigby Alex., 209 ; Giles, 188, 190, 224 ; Nic., 210
Riseley Nic., 93
Rob. f. Agnes, 18
—— f. Hanne, 18
—— f. Henr', 31, 33
—— f. Hugh, 31, 39
—— f. Math., 55, 58, 70
Rob. le Jewe, 72 ; Will., 73, 75, 76, 80, 86, 95
Robert (clerk), 46
Robinson Ad., 80 ; T., 210
Roby W., 83
Rochester Rob., 60
Roger (carpenter), 3
—— (merchant), 34

Roger f. Ewenild, 16
—— f. Ric., 12
Rome Ric., 18
Rose J., 173 ; T., 224 ; T. (sen.), 195, 205, 206
Ross Rog., 205, 206 ; T., 205, 206
Rovynton Emma, 17 ; Rob., 14, 17, 23b ; W., 21
    26, 27, 29
Rowland Eliz., 144 ; f. Eustas, Kt., 144
Russel Emma, 36 ; J., 203 ; Hen., 30, 45 ; Mart.
    57, 75, 80 ; W., 19
Ruyton Ric., 40
Ryding Chr., 162
Rymor Martin, 188 ; Peter, 188 ; T., 188

Sallay J., 100, 102, 103, 110, 114
Salvin J., 99
Scaresbreck H., 127
Scissor P., 4
Scot Ric., 95 ; W., 224
Seacome J., 208 ; Ra., 202, 208 ; Ric., 153 ; Rob.
    83, 108, 110, 114, 117
Secum T., 74, 202 ; W., 190, 193
Sedhead W. f. W., 7
Sefton J., 106 ; Matilda, 98, 123 ; Rob., 97 ; W., 6
Seton T., 54
Shakerley J., 57 ; J. fil Jord., 57
Sherburne Ric., 209
Sidgreves Em., 58, 67 ; Rog., 103
Simon (chaplain), 10
Singleton Rog., 162
Smerley W., 99
Somener J., 58, 59, 60, 61, 67, 69, 70
Somenour Ric., 23d
Sonky Rog., 23d
Southsex Ric., 28, 31, 33, 40
Sothworth Rob., 87, 89
Stalward Jordan (chaplain), 10
Stanay J., 61 ; Ric., 120, 121
Standish Edm. f. Jordan, 20, 27 ; Hugh, 15 ; J.
    47, 52 ; Laur., 131 ; Ra., 91, 95, 96 ; Hugh, 94
    Ric., 52, 171, 210, 213 ; T., 221 ; W., 20, 35, 38
    46 ; Rog., 38
Stanistreet Ric., 26
Stanley Alianora, 144 ; James, 143, 144, 145
    John, 130, 137 ; Sir Jas., 71 ; Sir John, 132
Strangeways Jas., 132
Starkie T., 222
St. Licio Gerard, 10
Stetheved W., 14
Stevenson T., 162
Stonbruglegh Tho. f. H., 62, 63
Stonbrigley W., 50
Sudale Rob., 173
Sulqui T., 9
Sutton Ric., 89
Swansey Rob., 180
Swyn Ric., 97, 98 ; W., 107, 109, 122
Swyneleys Ad., 13
Swindeley Rob., 151, 154
Swinley Rog., 7, 13, 23a, 23c ; W., 101, 102, 11
    125, 128

Taberner Ric., 165
Taillor Ric., 117
Tanner T., 35
Tarbock Edw., 224
Tarleton Hen., 71, 195
Tewe Ric., 42
Tho. f. Ad. f. Rob. (carp.), 34
—— f. Alan (plumber), 17
— - f. Brun., 2, 3
—— f. Ric., 22
—— f. Rob., 32
—— f. Rog., 12, 23b, 23c
Thomas J., 205, 206

Thomasson Hugh, 139 ; J., 205 ; Nic., 195
Thomson W., 162
Thornton Rog., 63
Tildesley H., 11*a*, 11*b* ; Nich., 14, 27
Tippup H., 92 ; J., 62, 63, 67, 103, 122 ; Ric., 64, 134
Tootell J., 210, 213 ; W., 210
Townley Ric., 94
Toxtaffe T., 188
Toxteth J., 158, 159 ; Jas., 159
Travers W., 212
Trewe Ric., 33
Trygg T., 96
Tue Ric., 70
Tunstal Hugh, 165
Turner Edw., 208
Twigg T., 116

Ustasmon Alan, 104
Uttings Ad. and Cecilia, 42

Vaughan Howell ap Jenn, 145

Vallbank T., 183
Valchemon W., 23*d*, 24, 39
Valens J., 5 ; Ric., 5
Valeton Ad. (rector), 23*c*
Valey Alex. f. Matt., 42
Valker A., 126, 148 ; Alm. f. Will., 73, 82 ; Alm. and Alice, 80 ; Rich., 12 ; Walt., 7
Vall Edward, 210
Valsemon Alan, 3, 8, 16, 68
Valshe Ste., 64, 69, 70
Valter (clerk), 45
Valt. the fuller, 12
Valton J., 106, 135 ; Ric., 4, 42 ; Rog., 149, 151, 171 ; Sim. f. Will., 50 ; Sim. and Alianora, 54
Vanton J., 203
Vareyn Laur., 124
Vebster Bryan, 199 ; Kath., 199 ; Rob., 199
Vestby W., 180
Vever T., 52
Vhalley Rob., 224
Vhite W., 223
Vhitfield Rob., 221

Whitling Jacob, 162 ; W., 162
Wigan Almeric, 72 ; Hen. f. Alm., 72, 73 ; Elnr. f. Nic., 19 ; Hen. f. Hugh, 21
Will. f. Ad. de Liverpool and Alice, 103, 120
—— f. Grun., 23*c*
—— f. Marg. and Alice, 46
—— f. Neel, 25
—— f. Ra., 8, 23*d*, 63
—— f. Ric., 1, 46, 50, 57
—— f. Rog. (cook), 131
—— f. Walt., 36, 37, 38, 41, 43, 45, 51
—— f. Walt. (fuller), 14, 17, 21, 29, 30
—— f. Will., 26, 29
—— (clerk), 4, 7, 23*a*
—— (currier), 25
—— (dyer), 30, 43, 45
—— (priest), 138
Williamson Rob., 212
Winstanley Edm., 157 ; H., 11*a*, 11*b*, 99 ; Jas., 179, 180 ; Ralph, 208, 210 ; Rog., 11*a*, 36 ; T., 224 ; W., 11*a*, 11*b*
Winterton Walt., 9
Wiswal Hugh and Margery, 55 ; J., 156 ; Ric., 156, 161
Wodeley T., 154
Wolton J., 142
Wolvesey H., 39
Wolveton Ad., 8
Woodfall J., 71
Woolfall Frances, 213
Woolton J., 67, 130
Woods J. and Alice, 149, 150, 151, 153
Woosey W. and R., 219
Workesley J. fil Rob., 124
Worshed W., 210
Worsley Hugh, 146 ; Marg., 192 ; Rob., 192
Worswell W., 214
Worthington Nich., 75, 76 ; Margaret, 78 ; Ric., 116 ; T., 83 ; W., 47, 52, 130, 209
Wroo J., 116
Wyke Gilb. f. Gilb., 20, 27
Wynd W., 75, 76, 78, 85, 95

Yate Ann, 213 ; Pet., 213, 217 ; Rog., 42 ; Sam., 213 ; Tho., 213

THOMAS BRAKELL LIMITED, LIVERPOOL.

www.ingramcontent.com/pod-product-compliance
Lightning Source LLC
Chambersburg PA
CBHW031451270326
41930CB00007B/941